Think Strategically

THINK
STRATEGICALLY

Xavier Gimbert
Associate Professor, Business Policy Department,
ESADE Business School

First published 2011 by
PALGRAVE MACMILLAN

Palgrave Macmillan in the UK is an imprint of Macmillan Publishers Limited, registered in England, company number 785998, of Houndmills, Basingstoke, Hampshire RG21 6XS.

Palgrave Macmillan in the US is a division of St Martin's Press LLC, 175 Fifth Avenue, New York, NY 10010.

Palgrave Macmillan is the global academic imprint of the above companies and has companies and representatives throughout the world.

Palgrave® and Macmillan® are registered trademarks in the United States, the United Kingdom, Europe and other countries.

ISBN 978–0–230–28487–6 hardback

This book is printed on paper suitable for recycling and made from fully managed and sustained forest sources. Logging, pulping and manufacturing processes are expected to conform to the environmental regulations of the country of origin.

A catalogue record for this book is available from the British Library.

A catalog record for this book is available from the Library of Congress.

10   9   8   7   6   5   4   3   2   1
20   19   18   17   16   15   14   13   12   11

Printed and bound in Great Britain by
CPI Antony Rowe, Chippenham and Eastbourne

To Bea, Laura and Sergi

Contents

LIST OF FIGURES

List of Figures

INTRODUCTION

Thinking is what sets human beings apart from the rest of the animal kingdom. And thinking is what distinguishes each individual human from all the others. We think differently, and that makes us different people, because it also makes us do things in a host of different ways. Companies differ too, due to the fact that they think differently and therefore act differently; their thinking is strategically different insofar as they follow a wide variety of strategies.

There is no denying that companies are different, and very much so, in what they own, the resources they possess (technology, know-how, intangibles such as the brand, money, buildings, facilities). However, if we are thinking about future competitive advantages, the most basic resource will be one that is not included in the list above: people. The above resources are certainly essential, but strategic thinking and the knowledge and skills of the people in the organization are what will lead on the company into the future. It is people who get the company moving. A powerful car with a bad driver will be overtaken by a less powerful one with a great driver, even if the first has a big lead.

This explains, for example, how Apple dethroned IBM when it spent 100 times less than its competitor on R&D. Business history is replete with examples of David slaying Goliath on the basis of his strategic ingenuity.

Rest assured: if you think strategically better than your competitors, your company will win the competitive battle in the mid or long term. No matter how superior your competitors may be today, no matter how substantial their resources may be at present, do not be discouraged. Think, think strategically. That is the essential resource. It doesn't cost money, but money can't buy it. It's the key.

The aim of this book is to help you think strategically. It explains simply and clearly the elements, concepts, analyses and interrelationships that make up this strategic thinking. Moreover, it offers thinking models as guides to this process.

Just as companies need to be different in order to achieve a competitive advantage, to have some characteristic feature that better matches their customers' needs, this book seeks to achieve the same. It has been written with the aim of being different from other books, to satisfy differently the need for knowledge of strategic management that is felt by entrepreneurs, managers and students of business administration at its various levels (undergraduate, MBA and executive programs).

From the start, this work has been conceived on the basis of a clear schema, a management model that is simple and straightforward to follow, each chapter being built on the foundation of the previous one. It provides easy explanations of the various strategic concepts and the complex interrelationships that exist between them. This is so because although the subject is complicated and dense it is set forth in such a way as to be up to date, didactic and clear. It contains constant references to companies and business situations. It also uses similes and metaphors that help the reader to understand each business perspective. It aims to be completely practical and useful, and, with this in mind, a series of questions for reflection are added at the end of each chapter. These questions are intended to facilitate the direct application to the company of the concepts, models and thoughts described in the body of the chapter.

In short, this book seeks to explain the keys to business management using a different style, a style that is easy to read, a world away from the typical tedious management handbooks, thus encouraging the reader to think about the fundamental concepts of company strategy.

This work is also an attempt to impart knowledge in a passionate way, by spreading the enthusiasm, the excitement and the thrill that is part and parcel of strategy. Strategic management has the capacity to change the direction of companies, it has the immense and wonderful power to transform, to innovate, to create. And remember that companies are the driving force behind the economy of countries and the world. As long ago as the mid-1990s, Richard Branson, creator and owner of Virgin, said: "People think politicians can change the world, but it's not true. The only people who have real power are us businesspeople." This is the strength of strategic management. Exciting stuff indeed!

This book is the result of more than 25 years of work by the author in the academic and business worlds. It is the consequence of his experience in both. It is also the fruit of his development as a writer and his reflections as an academic, manager and author, especially since 1998, when he published his first books[1] disseminating his first model of strategic thinking, the GIB (General, Integrative and Basic) model, of which this book presents a new development. This work includes his latest reflections and management models, the conclusions of his most recent papers,[2] and his answers to the new business world with which we must learn to live, in the wake of the deep economic and financial crisis of 2007–2011.

These personal visions and strategic models, together with the straightforward language with which the author confronts the complexity of strategy today, seek to endow this work with a distinctive hallmark. In the face of increasing complexity in the business environment, the answer is a clear and structured strategic vision of this complicated and confusing reality. Only in this way can it be subjected to the constant monitoring that this complexity demands.

CHAPTER I

Strategic Management, Strategic Levels and Processes

The working day was over; it was almost dinner time, but James still didn't have a minute to himself. He was general manager of a medium-sized company, and his diary, like those of his fellow executives, was practically full every day before work started. This situation was then complicated with the addition of the unforeseen circumstances that arose with terrifying frequency. The worldwide crisis of recent years exacerbated the picture even further, as it placed the company in a truly difficult position in which the entire management team had to be almost permanently in a state of absolute tension. When evening came, James felt a mixture of feelings: satisfaction at having overcome another day fraught with problems and at the same time distress at finding himself overwhelmed by events, at not being master of his own time.

There are a lot of Jameses, and not just because it is one of the commonest names in English, but also because one of the characteristics of today's executives is lack of time, the full diary. They are constantly absorbed in tasks and decisions that demand their full attention. If they do a poor job the company will feel the affect, its results will suffer, and in some cases the very future of the enterprise may be at risk. But are all these tasks and decisions part of strategic management? The answer is no. In fact, many of these tasks and decisions that focus the attention of general managers and management teams do not form part of strategic management.

It is crucial for entrepreneurs and senior managers to be conscious of what is really strategic, to realize what type of decisions can affect the future of their organization. Equally, it is essential for them to have a clear understanding of the different levels inherent in strategy and the consequences of this. And lastly, it is vital for them to be well acquainted with the different ways in which a strategic decision can be faced.

1.1 Operational Management and Strategic Management

When a manager is stressing and straining because a customer defaults on a large payment, a supplier has failed to deliver a key order, his information systems are down or there is a conflict between important members of his team, is he managing strategically? Much as these are important problems, and much as they all have to be solved as quickly as possible so that the business can operate normally and its results are not adversely affected, these problems do not belong to the realm of strategic management. They are all operational problems – which does not mean they are any the less important, as has already been emphasized above.

Operational problems are so important that a company can go under if they are not properly addressed. This is why operational management absorbs almost all the hours in a working day; they are not easy to solve, but unless they are solved the future of the organization may be jeopardized.

So what differences are there between strategic and operational management? There are several, and they define a clear dividing line between the two types of management. One very obvious difference is that operational management is a short-term approach; hence it is often described as "day-to-day management". Operational problems arise today and require an immediate solution to prevent them from affecting the organization. Think of the four examples mentioned above: we cannot leave a company for very long without cash, supplies or information systems, or with clashes among staff. All these problems arise suddenly and demand immediate attention and solutions.

Strategic management, on the other hand, is by definition a long-term approach. It seeks to ensure that the company will continue to be competitive over a long period of time, fitting into its environment better than its competitors for years. Logically the length of this "long" period of time depends on the type of strategic decision concerned, as we will see throughout this book. We can make strategic decisions on a time scale of one, three, five or even twenty years or more. Obviously, the longer the time scale of the strategic decision the more difficult it is to analyze the environment; the decision is increasingly out of focus and our vision of its key features is more and more blurred.

Because of this, strategic decisions are usually made for a period of just a few years, and the strategy adopted is reviewed at least annually, or more often if there are unforeseen changes in the environment. However, it is also true that some strategic decisions are made for a horizon of many years hence, for example the development of a new model of aircraft (the case of Airbus when they decided to stake their future on the A-380, the commercial aircraft with the largest seating capacity in history). Also there are decisions that are difficult to go back on; for example, investments in R&D or marketing allocations to position a new product are lost if we subsequently decide to change strategy.

Another difference between operational and strategic management is that the former usually has a functional and introverted vision of the company. If we think back to the four operational examples mentioned earlier, each of them belongs to a functional area and looks inside the company. The examples mentioned can easily be pigeonholed in a particular functional area; to be exact, they belong to finance, operations, information systems and human resources.

In contrast, in the case of strategic management the vision is general, over the whole of the company, and also extroverted; instead of only looking inside the company, it also looks outwards at its surroundings. Strategic management requires a vision of all the areas, because although on occasion it might seem to focus on one functional area, it always needs to bear in mind the other areas. For example, if we have to decide what sort of product to make in the future, this decision is undeniably in the area of operations. However, marketing has to tell us whether the product has a sufficient number of potential customers; whether it is really going to satisfy a market need. And R&D may have to develop the product. And human resources must always provide the necessary personnel to make it. And finance must ensure that the company will be able to fund the whole process and make a profit from it. Strategic management has an overview of the entire company because all its areas are strategically interrelated, as this book will demonstrate and highlight.

Strategic management is also extrovert because it looks outwards at the environment as well as inwards at the company. Strategic management is no more than the process of constant adaptation of the company to its environment, in order always to be better than its competitors in some vital aspect that is valued by its customers. In this definition two key strategic players are to be found in the outside world.

The customer, the final object of the strategy, forms part of this outside world. The customer's needs often change, so the strategy must observe this possible mutation tirelessly. Competition, that terrible obstacle that strategy has to overcome, is also in the outside world. Competitors complicate the strategic game in that they make the game change from one of absolute values, such as "being good", to one of relative values, such as "being better". My strategy is good insofar as it is better than that of my competitors, insofar as it fits our environment better. This is a daunting change, because it complicates matters. You can be sure of an absolute value; you can be sure of being good, average or bad. But it is very difficult to be sure of a relative value, because "the other", the competition in this case, is always striving to improve. Lastly, the macro-environment, the economic, social, political, legal and technological setting, which also has a profound influence on strategy (we need only recall the terrible crisis of 2007–2011), is also in the outside world.

As we will see presently, this is a crucial point, as we will never be able to predict for sure how the environment will evolve. What will inflation be in our country and that of our competitors two or three years from now? Will we be in a period of economic growth or will there be a recession? What technologies will appear? What buying habits will change? Who will be our main competitors? What strategies will they follow? These are examples of questions that can be vital for the strategic management of a business. They all refer to the outside world. And all of them are unpredictable in the long run.

This last characteristic leads us on to another feature which is no less important. If strategic management depends on the environment and the environment changes rapidly and unpredictably, every time we think strategically we are facing a different environment from the one we faced last time. So if we reached a strategic decision that was right then, this does not mean in the slightest that the same decision would be right today. Therefore strategic decisions cannot usually be repeated, and their expiry date tends to be very short.

On the other hand, a good operational decision can be repeated successfully if we are faced with the same problem further down the line. If, for example, a supply shortage is solved by looking for alternative suppliers with similar value for money, or by successfully replacing some of the components, these solutions could be repeated in a future case in which the problem crops up again.

Because operational management is short-term, it works with quantitative data, exact data. To return to the examples above, we know whether a customer has defaulted on 30,000, 300,000 or 1 million euros; or whether the supply shortage prevents us from manufacturing 50, 500 or 5000 units. We have exact data because these are today's problems. In strategic management we will always be working with more qualitative data, or with approximate quantitative data. The certainty of the data will never be absolute because we will be thinking in the long term, setting up scenarios and hypotheses. As we have been shown often enough, no one can tell the future.

So far we have described the differences between operational and strategic management. We have described the various factors that perfectly delimit each of these types of decision-making. However, we have yet to deal with the fundamental difference between these two sorts of management. As we said earlier, they are both very difficult to get right: companies perish not only for strategic reasons but also for operational ones, for not managing day-to-day affairs well enough, for not solving quickly and efficiently the problems that arise. In short, both require very well trained and responsible managers.

However, operational management has one great advantage over the strategic kind. In operational management problems are identified. They come and look for us and expect an answer. The executive is in his office, the phone rings or a colleague turns up, and the problem is identified. The executive is informed of the fact that a customer has failed to pay a large sum of money, a supplier has not delivered a key order, the information systems are down or there is a clash between important members of the organization (to use the examples of operational problems mentioned earlier). The executive must have sufficient training to solve these problems, but they have been perfectly identified. In a word, operational management is reactive. It is a matter of reacting.

Quite the opposite is true of strategic management. Strategic problems never identify themselves; strategic problems never knock on the door. If the executive does not discover them, if the executive does not think about them, by the time they identify themselves, by the time the first outcomes of the strategic problem arise, it is usually too late. In a word, strategic management is proactive. It is the company's responsibility to be one step ahead of the future in order to prepare for that same future. It is up to the company to think about whether its customers are changing. It must be on the lookout for the strategic movements of its competitors. It must sense whether there is going to be a crisis or any other drastic economic change.

Neither customers nor competitors nor the economy call to say that they are going to change and that the company should get ready for these changes. This is the fundamental difference between strategic and operational management. It is not a case of thinking what decision I am going to make tomorrow, but rather what decision I should make today in order to achieve what I want tomorrow. The sobering fact is that, as we have already mentioned, if I wait until tomorrow to make a decision it will usually be too late.

1.2 Strategic Levels

Within strategy we find different levels. They are all crucial for the future of the organization, but each offers its own perspective, involving different types of decisions, since each addresses totally different issues. As is shown in Figure 1.1, these strategic levels are the corporate, the business and the functional.

Logically, if a company is engaged in only one activity it will only have the business and functional levels. The corporate level will only appear in diversified enterprises, companies that are engaged in more than one business. As we will see, in the case of diversified companies the mission and vision differ in each of the company's businesses. In these cases the planning process is carried out at the business level. This is obvious if we think that each of the corporation's businesses has a different environment (macro-environment, industry, competition or market), and the corporation has a different competitive position in each of them.

While this is true, it is also true that in diversified enterprises there are processes, concepts and analyses that can also have a cross-perspective. This cross-perspective gives rise to corporate strategy.

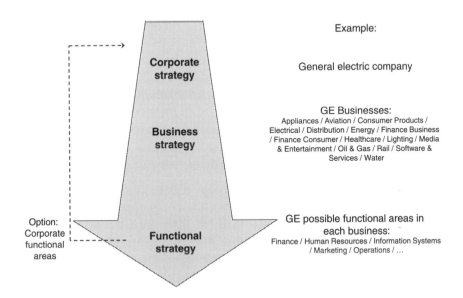

Figure 1.1 The priority of the three strategic levels: GE example of the three levels

1.2.1 Corporate Strategy

Corporate strategy has responsibility over four main types of decisions.

- **Influence over business strategy.** Corporate strategy defines a way of doing things that must be respected by the other levels. For example, if a corporation decides to follow a low-cost strategy, this must be incorporated into the strategies of all the group's business units. This is the case of the easy group, with low-cost businesses such as easyJet, easyCar and easyHotel, among others.

- **Deciding about what businesses the group should operate in.** The second major corporate responsibility is to decide what businesses the group should be involved in: which it should enter and which it should leave. Only those individuals who have an overview of the whole organization can assess the expected mid- and long-term profitability of each business, what each of them contributes to the rest and the synergies it produces.

  Sometimes a company has two businesses in one. When in September 2009 the Accor group decided to sell the buildings of its 158 low-cost hotels (Formule 1) in France (for €272 million) and manage them on a rental basis, they were in fact separating two businesses, the hotel business and the property business, and getting rid of the latter in the case of its lower-end French hotels (with an average price per room of €33 in 2009). This disinvestment in the property business enabled the Accor group to reduce its net debt by €187 million in 2009 and so produce a positive impact of around €5 million on its profits before tax. In fact, companies that own the premises used in their businesses often treat them as an independent business unit; this is the only way to know the real profitability of each business, since if they do not the profitability of one can disguise the losses of the other.

- **Investment of resources.** A group exists as such because its proprietors – its shareholders – own the companies it comprises (or at least they own a large part of them). Therefore, the prime interest of the corporate level is to improve the profitability of the group as a whole. Only this level can decide how to invest the group's resources, as mentioned earlier, according to the expected profitability of the different activities and what each of them contributes to the rest. On the basis of this overall estimate, the corporate level must decide how to distribute its financial, human and technical capabilities, knowledge, and tangible and intangible assets among its various businesses. In fact, the corporate level may decide to transfer all the profits of one business to another, or indeed most of the capabilities of one business (people, assets) to another.

■ **Creation of synergies.** The fourth corporate responsibility is to ensure that the group is worth more than just the sum of its businesses. A group that is worth the sum of what each of its businesses is worth on its own has failed as a group. For the whole to be worth more than just the sum of its parts, it is important to exploit synergies between businesses. And these synergies can be forthcoming through two different but complementary channels.

The first of these channels appears when we use the corporate level to observe the functional level. In this way we discover that each functional area is repeated in each business. This may lead the corporation to reflect whether a transverse view might have a contribution to make. And the answer might be yes. There might be certain activities – information systems or management control, for example – in which we realize that one single department could serve for all the businesses in the group. If this is the case there may be a large saving to be made, as the same activity can be performed, with adaptations, just once for all the units instead of being repeated. We can have a single person in charge of the activity who will have an overview of all the businesses and will perform it for all of them (introducing minor adaptations if necessary).

This transverse view may enable us to perform the function better. For example, in the case of human resources, we may discover that there are people with potential in one business but without a future there because the business has no position of responsibility available. These people can move to a different business where there are jobs available with a future. Or in the area of finance, we might discover that whereas one business has a lack of liquidity in another there is surplus cash, and that the one with liquid assets can direct this money to the one that is running short. The former will charge the latter interests, but these interests will remain within the group.

At the same time, by having a transverse area we are cutting costs, as its budget is divided among the group's various businesses. If this is possible, what the group is doing in effect is to move one functional area up to the corporate level. This area will be both functional (because it performs a function) and corporate (because it is performed jointly for all the businesses). Logically, it is not always possible to perform an activity in this way, but all groups should consider this possibility, always taking into account the possible coordination problems that might also arise.

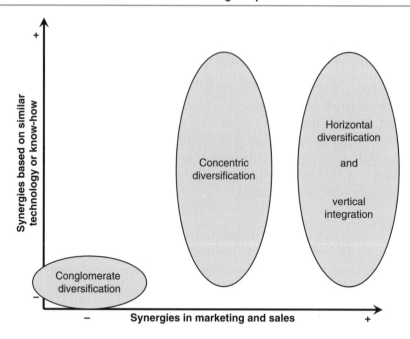

Figure 1.2 Diversification: possible synergies and types of diversification

The second way of obtaining synergies in a group is to have related businesses. This is when a corporation is made up of businesses that display likenesses, either because the technology or know-how of some of them is similar or because they have the same or similar customers. In such cases, when the group starts up a new business it is not starting from zero, but from knowledge it already possessed. Furthermore, when it is developed and maintained, there is always a transfer of knowledge among the various businesses that is constantly reinforced. Different forms of diversification arise as a result of the variety of relationships that can exist between businesses. They are based on the different types of synergies that can be achieved. In this way, as we see in Figure 1.2, the four types of diversification appear.[1]

In *horizontal diversification* the businesses have the same customers (but logically meet different needs of those customers). This would be the case of a chain of hypermarkets that also offers its customers the services of a travel agency. In this type of diversification the synergies in marketing and sales are huge, since the customers are the same. The group's knowledge of them serves for all the businesses; the loyalty won in one business can be taken advantage of in others.

In *vertical integration* it is the company itself that becomes either customer or supplier in the new business. This would be the case, for example, if the chain of hypermarkets bought up one of its suppliers of dairy products. In that case the synergies are obvious. However, in vertical integration it is important to bear in mind that the corporation is taking an increased risk, as all the integrated businesses have the same end consumer. Think, for example, of a clothes manufacturer that also owns shops; if a winter is mild and clothing sales drop, both of the businesses (manufacturing and distribution) will suffer the hardships of low sales.

Conglomerate diversification is the only type of diversification that does not present any synergies, as by definition it has none, either due to similarity of technology or know-how or due to customer similarity. This could be the case of a group that owns one company in the food industry and another in property promotion and sales.

In the last type, *concentric diversification*, some synergy is created, either because the customers of the new business are similar (but not the same, as then it would be horizontal diversification) or because it shows a certain similarity of technology or know-how, or indeed for both reasons, as could be the case with car and motorcycle manufacturing, which gives rise to both types of synergy.

1.2.2 Business Strategy

The second strategic level (or the first if the company is not diversified and has only one business) is the business level. Earlier we mentioned the easy group, with the examples easyJet, easyCar and easyHotel; each of these three companies has its own strategy, despite the fact that they are related businesses and enjoy obvious synergies. The industries formed by airlines (easyJet), car hire (easyCar) and hotels (easyHotel) are very different. Each of these companies in the easy group aims at customers with different needs, faces different competitors, has different suppliers, and so on. We can say exactly the same about the example of the chain of hypermarkets that also offers its customers the services of a travel agency or owns its supplier of dairy products.

If each of these businesses has different customers, competitors and suppliers, obviously their strategies will follow independent analysis and planning processes and the end result of these processes will be different: the competitive position of these companies in each business may differ.

The main responsibility of the business strategy is, as we have already mentioned, to obtain a competitive advantage for the company in the industry; to enable it to be better than its competitors in some essential aspect, at least for a sufficient number of customers to keep the company going. This is precisely what we will relate in the following chapters of this book, all of which refer to this level of business strategy.

1.2.3 Functional Strategy

Just as each business within a group of enterprises must think out and decide on its strategy, each functional area (marketing, operations, finance, etc.) within a business must think and decide about its own strategies. The perspective of a functional area is totally different from the corporate or the business perspective. The corporate level, as we have seen, thinks and decides about businesses. The business level analyzes and decides about how to obtain a competitive advantage in a particular industry, about how to satisfy its customers better than the competition. The functional level has a much more specific vision, in much sharper focus.

For example, the area of marketing focuses mainly on the market, getting to know the company's customers, getting acquainted with their different needs, and properly communicating the messages and positioning that the company decides on and wants to convey. In turn, the area of finance concentrates on economic and financial aspects, liquid assets, ratios and so on. And the area of human resources deals with people. Again we see how different levels of strategy provide different visions and consequently different types of strategic decisions. They are strategic decisions because the future of the company depends on them too. No matter how good its business strategy, no company can survive unless its marketing, human resources and finance strategies are effective, among other things because the business strategy takes shape through these functional strategies.

Logically, the various functional strategies must work in the same direction as the business strategy, and therefore they must all be consistent with one another. Otherwise we might find that the sum of several very good strategies at a functional level is a resounding failure for the company as a whole. For example, a business strategy that is committed to cutting costs and standardizing the product in operations is incompatible with a marketing strategy that pursues elitist differentiation, no matter how well designed it is.

1.3 Planned versus Emergent Strategy

This last section addresses one of the mostly hotly debated issues in strategic management: how strategy can be decided.[2] Planning can be defined as the process whereby strategy is decided, by analyzing both the inner workings and the outside environment of the company and evaluating the alternatives that arise from that analysis. This definition leads us to a way of thinking out and deciding on strategy: the planned strategy pioneered by Igor Ansoff and other authors.[3] In this approach, strategy is decided by means of a rational, formalized, systematic, planned process. It is analyzed stage by stage, then several alternatives are evaluated, and finally the whole strategy is decided for a relatively long period of time. But there are many other ways of performing a process of strategic decision, in addition to this rational, formalized, systematic, planned mode.

Those authors who criticize such a highly planned process hold that it fails to fit into such a changing and unpredictable reality as we face today.[4] This rational and formalized way of operating deprives the company of capacity to react, as there are occasions when it does not have the necessary time to make decisions in this way. This critical vision leads to another way of making strategic decisions, the opposite extreme.

This is what is known as emergent strategy, a more incremental, cumulative and intuitive way of thinking out and deciding on strategy: informal, unplanned processes in which the choices appear in response to unforeseen changes in the environment. We can sum up these two extremes in the words of Henry Mintzberg:[5] one way leads to strategy through planning, the other through learning. Figure 1.3 depicts these two ways of deciding on strategy, these two main channels. In planned strategy we observe

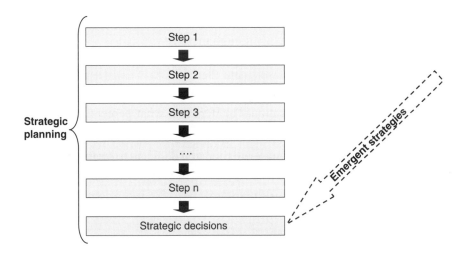

Figure 1.3 Planned strategy and emergent strategy

a step-by-step process, while emergent strategies are a constant flow of decisions in response to changes in the environment.

Ansoff and Mintzberg, the main representatives of these two schools of thought, became embroiled in public discussions on the advantages of their respective points of view and the shortcomings of those of their adversaries.[6] However, both channels lead to strategy. And both channels are necessary, depending on the moment, the circumstances of the environment and the competitive position of the company and its industry.

In fact, as many authors have stressed,[7] strategy is a mixture of both visions. In the real world companies decide their strategy in both ways, sometimes planning the future in advance and engaging in profound analyses, reflections and debates, and sometimes reacting in an emergent fashion, immediately counteracting sudden changes brought about by their competitors, customers or the economic environment.

The crux of the matter is that, whatever road the company chooses to follow when deciding its strategy, it will always need knowledge and understanding both of strategic concepts and of a model of thinking that is capable of bringing together and interrelating these concepts. Any model of strategic thinking can be used in planned strategy, as a set of guidelines for this formal and rational process. However, it is also useful to be familiar with it in emergent strategy, in this case as a mental model or mindset. Knowledge of the key strategic concepts and how they are interrelated helps to provide a prompt understanding of the changing conditions of the environment and to respond to them more rapidly.

1.4 Questions for Reflection

  I. Take a look at your monthly diary. What percentage of your time is spent attending to operational matters and what percentage is given over to strategic matters?

 II. What can you do to increase the time you dedicate to strategic matters or thinking about the strategic position of your company?

III. Is your company diversified? If so, in what businesses? If the answer is yes:

   a. What types of diversifications has your company followed?

b. What strategic logic do these diversifications follow? Are there strategic interrelationships among the various businesses?

c. Does the group take advantage of corporate synergies?

IV. Are formal strategic planning processes conducted in your company? If so, how often (yearly, twice yearly, etc.)?

V. Are you satisfied with your answer to the above question? Will you act differently in future?

VI. When major unforeseen changes occur in the environment (competitors, customers, the economy), does your company react appropriately? Is it capable of realizing emergent strategy?

VII. How could you improve your strategic response to unforeseen changes in the environment?

CHAPTER 2

Key Strategic Concepts

The first thing companies – like people – have to do if they want to improve is to gain an insight into where they are starting from, what they are like, what they are doing, what they do well and what could be improved. Consequently, any strategic planning process at business level must start with a profound knowledge of the current state of the firm's key strategic concepts. Defining this is stage zero of a process of strategic thinking and decision-making.

The purpose of this book is not only to describe all the necessary concepts and analyses to think and decide about the strategy of the company (providing models to this end) but also to constantly interrelate these concepts and analyses. In fact, the logic of the models presented in this book is to maintain this constant interrelation.

Our intention is to establish this interrelation right from this first step, from this thinking about key strategic concepts. To do so, we will present these concepts in a structured fashion, as if they were pieces of a sculpture.[1] We first lay a foundational concept (the values of the organization) and place the rest on top in succession, as shown in Figure 2.1.

We will explain and interrelate these key concepts following the logic of building this sculpture. The order in which we place each concept, its distribution within the sculpture, will help us to understand its function, its importance and its relationship with the rest of the concepts.

2.1 Values

Values define how the organization wants to act and behave, which roads it wants to take and which it does not. They specify the nature of the

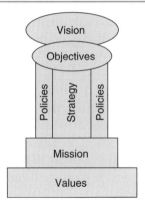

Figure 2.1 Key strategic concepts presented in sculpture form

Source: A. Vilanova

relationships between the individuals who comprise the company and how the company relates to its customers, its suppliers, the community in which it operates, and so on. They are based on beliefs as to what is desirable, valuable, justifiable. Values should mobilize and amplify the energies of an organization, and therefore they should be understood and shared.

The values of a firm are imposed by its owners, its shareholders, not its managers. A company belongs to its owners; it is their money that is at stake, and it is they who will define what values it is going to have. A conservative owner will never allow his managers to implement an aggressive strategy that might have a high rate of return but puts his assets at risk. No matter how good that strategy is, it will not be accepted, because it goes against the values of the conservative ownership. Similarly, ethical shareholders will not tolerate the company managers going beyond certain lines of behavior.

Hence values are the only concept that does not change after a process of strategic thinking. Values do not change, unless the company changes owners. When a firm is sold, taken over or merged, its shareholding structure changes. In these cases the new owners do not usually have the same values as the old ones, and so the values are transformed. Values can also change if a succession occurs in a family firm: the new generation that takes over does not necessarily have exactly the same values as the previous one.

In large corporations, organizations that usually have many thousands of shareholders, values – like the other key concepts – are the jurisdiction of those who hold power, those who dominate the board of directors.

Thus managers should reconcile themselves with the values of the company for which they work. If they do not share them they will not be at ease doing their job and they will end up leaving the company, or at least that would be the best solution.

If we take a look at Figure 2.1 we find that the company's values are at the base of the sculpture. Therefore, this strategic concept influences the rest, it delimits them, it channels them in a certain direction. The values of a company will color the rest of its key concepts. This tallies with the definition of values given at the beginning of this section: values tell us how the company wants to act, how it wants to behave, which roads it wants to follow and which it does not.

And, whether we are an enterprise or an individual, not only do we reach decisions on the basis of our values, depending on whether we are ethical or unethical, conservative or aggressive, paternalistic, perfectionist and so on, but we also make decisions according to our analysis of the situation. And as we will see in the following chapters, analyzing the environment is fundamental in a strategic thinking process.

We interpret the environment according to our values. The same reality is seen differently according to each person's values. A glance at the range of newspapers available to us is enough to make this plain. Some facts are interpreted very differently according to the ideological leanings of each newspaper. There is only one reality, but many interpretations. This can be seen clearly in politics, but also in sport. The same tackle is seen as a penalty by the supporters of one team, whereas in the eyes of their rivals the penalty is pure invention.

In short, a company's values cause it to interpret and analyze the environment differently. And this makes it decide differently. Values influence both of the key processes in strategic thinking: analysis and decision-making. That is why they form the foundation in Figure 2.1.

Values cause us to reach decisions in a particular way, but while some values could be called non-negotiable (such as being ethical or having risk aversion), there may be another sort of decision that a company is obliged to make against its values. For example, Nicolas Hayek, the entrepreneur responsible for the astonishing resurgence of the Swiss watch industry in the 1980s, with success stories like the creation of Swatch, had among his values a strong sense of nationalism; he felt very Swiss. As a result, he strongly desired that his country should maintain its technological and industrial independence, and so he attached great value to his watches continuing to be manufactured in Switzerland. When he launched Swatch, a low-cost watch, strategic logic told him that if the watches were manufactured in Asian countries they would have lower costs. However, because of his values, he was determined to manufacture them in his own country. This led him to follow an inverse process, first fixing the selling price and then subtracting from this the margin he wanted to make and the distribution and communication costs (shipping, storage, advertising, and marketing). This gave him the cost of the operations ... and from here he went on to design a product and a production system that would allow him to manufacture with those costs in Switzerland.

This case can bring us to reflect on the possible inapplicability of some values. The fact that Mr Hayek held the values described above urged him strongly to manufacture in Switzerland, which he achieved because it is a country with a long tradition and know-how in this type of product (and also with country differentiation, as a result of which the "made in Switzerland" label meant that the consumer would pay a little more). However, let's imagine that his inverse process of thinking had led him to the conclusion that it was impossible to manufacture in Switzerland at lower costs. His business intelligence, his entrepreneurial spirit (another value), would have advised him to subordinate his value of patriotism to the viability of the new business project he had created.

Although, as we have already stressed, values are vital in a process of strategic thinking, they tend to be left out of this process. It is very common to start a strategic process with the next concept, neglecting corporate values. But leaving them out does not mean escaping their influence. It is therefore advisable to be conscious of the company's values when thinking about strategy. We won't be able to change them, but we will be aware of their influence.

Another issue is when the true values of the firm are not expressed. If we take a look at the values that companies convey to their market we will see that many are along the lines of being ethical, protecting the environment, caring about their employees, being customer-oriented, contributing to society, working in a team and so on. Words that are often repeated when talking about values include integrity, respect, equity, transparency, mutual benefit, control, independence . . . .

Of course they may be absolutely true. No doubt they are true in almost all cases. However, there may be cases in which they are not. If this hypothesis is valid and there are companies that communicate values that they do not actually possess, we can say two things. First, such organizations are defining what sort of values they have by deceiving their market with this message. And second, this message does not belong to the concept of values but rather the area of marketing, as it is simply a communication tool that is being used by the company to be seen in a particular way (which in fact is not true).

2.2 Mission

The mission should state exactly what the company does, the nature of its business. We cannot begin to analyze the environment or think about corporate strategy or any other key concept unless we are quite clear about what the company does. This is why the mission is the next concept that we put in place in the sculpture of key concepts that we are building, as shown in Figure 2.1.

One way of stating the mission is through Abell's business concept.[2] By means of three questions, this model specifies the exact business in which the company is engaged:

- **What** need does it attempt to satisfy? (Type of need)

- **Who** is it aimed at? (Market segment/s)

- **How** does it do it? (Technology or know-how)

Let us consider two of the big Detroit car firms, General Motors and Chrysler. If we wanted to define their mission, their business concept, up to summer 2009 we could say it was to satisfy the need for transport at speed, with power and plenty of room; of customers with a certain amount of purchasing power and who valued this roominess, strength and speed; through powerful engines and large, sturdy cars. Unquestionably, not all their customers (or their cars) were the same; there were different segments within this business definition. But these three answers defined what these companies did.

So, the mission defines the nature of a company's business, what it does. It also provides three channels for thinking about the future, an essential element in a thinking process in which thought is precisely what we should be maximizing. A firm can decide to change the needs it wishes to satisfy, or it can aim at different customers, just as it can do its business differently, with different technology or know-how. Or it can decide to change two of these strategic lines at the same time, or it can even change all three simultaneously.

If a company defines its mission using Abell's business concept, it ensures that it has more than just a product (or service) vision. Consequently, it will not die with its product (or service), as it would if it defined its mission solely on the basis of that vision. For example, a company might define itself as a manufacturer and installer of glass wool and rock wool (mineral fibers for insulation). If this product is mature and the market is gradually replacing it with synthetic materials like polyurethane, this firm will die with its product. However, if instead of adopting this product-oriented definition it defines itself according to the business concept, it will do so as a company that satisfies insulation needs, for construction and promotion firms, using glass wool and rock wool. That way, when it sees that the product it is using is being replaced by another one, it will change its "how", keeping the same "what" and "who".

Therefore, by using Abell's business concept, a company will have greater vision and strategic flexibility, thus avoiding the terrible product/service orientation that has had such disastrous consequences for so many companies – like Kodak, who continued to concentrate on conventional rolls of film even as digital technology was being developed.

As well as defining what the company does and giving it greater flexibility and possibility of change, the mission should make the organization think about its viability. On stating its mission, a company might realize that it has – or is going to have – an outdated business model. And if this is the case, the only thing left to find out is when the inevitable bankruptcy will take place.

In summer 2009, why was Barack Obama's government so reluctant to invest the US taxpayers' money in Detroit car firms? Perhaps because they made cars almost no one wanted any more. Perhaps because their business model had become outdated and they could only survive by reinventing themselves. Hence the bankruptcies of first Chrysler and then General Motors, and their subsequent transformation, through new business models, into smaller and more efficient companies. Had they not done so, a multi-million dollar injection would have had the same effect as a blood transfusion on a corpse.

The Detroit automobile corporations were a prime example of how fundamental it is to have a good business model as a condition for survival. If the model is outdated, nothing can be done. If the mission is not competitive, nothing else matters. There's no point in worrying about the rest of the key strategic concepts. We're going to fail anyway. In 2008 and 2009, after the virulent global crisis unleashed at the end of 2007, car users – even American ones – no longer wanted big, strong, robust fast cars, as they could no longer pay for the inordinate amount of petrol such cars consume. As a result, the Detroit companies found that their "who" had disappeared, because their "what" no longer existed and their "how" was completely obsolete. Hence the bankruptcy of Chrysler and General Motors, and hence their (partial) resurrection could only be accompanied by a new mission, a new business model.

Or we might find the opposite: that the business definition is enough to ensure a competitive advantage. But unfortunately this is a rare exception to the rule. When the business model is absolutely innovative, as was the case, for example, of Dell, Amazon and Swatch when they started out, the mission itself, the actual business definition, is the company's greatest competitive advantage. Since it is innovative, the company generates an environment that comes close to a monopoly, because no other company has the same business definition at that stage.

However, in most cases an appropriate business definition is merely a necessary but insufficient condition. Usually a company is forced to compete, within that definition, with others, all struggling to attract the same customers by satisfying similar needs in a similar way. This is when it needs to find a competitive advantage through strategy: to be better than the rest of the companies in the industry in some aspect that is appreciated by its customers. Typically, the mission describes the ring in which all the companies with the same mission fight it out to have the best competitive advantage. This is why the strategic thinking process must continue after the key concepts have been thought about and defined. The company must seek a competitive advantage, fighting against other companies with the same mission, in the same business.

2.3 Vision

We have seen above how the mission is essential because it defines what the company does. But as we know, the business world is totally dynamic; it changes every second. We also know that the primordial function of strategic management is to be ahead of that change. And our definition of the mission means that we are talking about today, what the company does now, the nature of our current business. In short, we need to introduce the future, the long term, into the perspective we have with the mission. This need gives rise to the vision.

The vision enables us to think about what we want to be but are not (yet). This is crucial because a company needs direction, it needs to know where it wants to get. Its vision must provide it with this orientation, this meaning to what it does. Hence in the sculpture we are making (see Figure 2.1) vision is on top. It represents where the firm wants to end up, by accomplishing its mission on the basis of its values.

But for the vision to be truly valid and guide a company toward its future, it must be a challenge. A vision should motivate, it should be capable of raising an organization up from its failures. It must give every person who belongs to an organization a component of ambition. It must provide each of its members with a strong will to overcome. So it has to be a challenge, ambitious but attainable.

Therefore a utopian vision is absolutely no good to anyone. No one will believe in it, it will not motivate, it will not put across so much as an ounce of ambition. The same happens with a vision that is too easy to achieve, one that fails to constitute a challenge. It too will be unable to motivate, to muster that ambition that moves winning companies.

Increasingly, business reality shows us that successful companies are those that are made up of passionate people. The passion with which they work moves mountains; it provides such indispensable elements nowadays as initiative, creativity and the will to overcome. Therefore, vision is an essential concept if we wish to transform an organization, to make it better and better. A united management team providing cohesion for the whole organization, causing information and knowledge to flow through all the layers and areas of the company, where everyone learns from everyone, working with passion and transmitting these qualities to all the collaborators, is practically unbeatable.

One of the advantages of the vision as regards empowering the capacity for motivation and ambition is that it has no date attached to it. Visions such as "we will be the best company in the industry" or "to dominate the world market" can be assumed more easily, can be more believable, since they have no expiry date. If the organization really believes in it, if it is really convinced that it can be the best in the industry or dominate the world market, no matter how distant that vision of reality lies, it will provide the company with an extraordinary strength that will enable it to move in that direction and get better and better.

For an organization that is out in front, the "we will continue to be leaders" type of vision is equally powerful. This is an extremely strong vision, as it is effectively saying to the competition: "do whatever you like; we'll carry on being leaders", or in other words, "you'll never catch up with us". As we all know, it is even more difficult to stay at the top than it is to get to the top, so a vision of this type provides a leading organization with additional doses of motivation.

By definition, when a vision is accomplished it ceases to be a vision, as it ceases to define what the company wants to become, what it wants to achieve. In fact, once achieved, what used to be the vision comes to form part of the mission, of what the company is.

Sometimes companies state their mission and their vision together. We may find corporate mission statements that set forth the nature of their company's business (mission) in conjunction with their vision of the future, with what they want to be (vision). In such cases, these two concepts are merged into a single definition.

2.4 Objectives

In the above, we have defined vision as a concept that allows the company to think about what it wants to be, what it wants to attain, in the future. It is the concept that provides direction, enables it to know where it wants to go. But all this could also be said of a company's objectives. Objectives also look to the future; they too enable us to think about what we want to achieve. So what is the difference between vision and objectives?

Objectives have one clear difference from the vision, namely that they are quantifiable. Furthermore, they are quantifiable in two ways: time and the goal pursued. An objective always implies time. It is to be achieved in six months, or one, three or five years; it always includes a temporal component. And it always entails a specific goal to be reached. Achieving sales of €500 million, a 1 percent increase in market share, or increase in sales of 10 percent, or a 15 percent cut in costs, penetrating two new countries, or entering a new market, are all examples of specific goals.

Objectives can be regarded as the concrete form taken by the vision; for this reason, in the sculpture we are building (see Figure 2.1) the objectives are located underneath the company's vision. Normally a vision will be broken down into several objectives over time. If, for example, the company's vision is "to dominate the world market", this vision will be broken down into annual objectives such as "next year we must move into three new countries" or "increase our worldwide share by 0.3 percent". In this way, new objectives take shape yearly and lead the company on toward achieving its vision.

This is the contribution of objectives. They are specific goals, and they are measurable and controllable, which makes them easier to carry out. They increase the organization's commitment, both collectively and individually, as they provide the people who comprise it with a sense of direction. They are a guide for action, they help to establish priorities, by focusing the energy of management and indeed the whole company, thus legitimizing resource allocation.

Since they are measurable, they help to control and evaluate results; they are standards, yardsticks, for the actions of the company (even qualitative objectives include a measurable component, although, depending how this is measured, there may be a certain degree of subjectivity).

We can apply the same reasoning to objectives as we did to vision, insofar as they need to constitute a challenge, without being utopian. As objectives are a concretion of the vision in the form of specific goals on a particular time scale, the previous reasoning is equally valid. Only a set of objectives that pose a challenge will motivate, will provide the necessary component of ambition and eagerness to face the difficult moments that the organization will go through before it achieves them. Only this sort of objectives will guard against the enterprise losing vitality.

2.5 Strategy

This entire process of thinking is about strategy; strategy is the subject of this whole book. We can say that strategy is the way in which the company attains its competitive advantage; it is its way of competing, of being better than its rivals at satisfying its customers' key needs. Each strategic perspective will provide a vision of strategy; each analysis will lead us to a type of strategic decision, a way of competing.

Now that we are defining the key concepts, now that we are using them to build a sculpture that reasons these definitions out and explains how they are interrelated, we can say that strategy is the way a company has of achieving its vision and objectives on the basis of its mission and in keeping with its values. Therefore, if we go back to the picture of the sculpture in Figure 2.1, strategy connects the base, formed by values and mission, to the upper part, made up of vision and objectives.

As we have just said, the rest of this book, the rest of the thinking process, is pure strategy. Each stage of the process will lead us to a strategic perspective, each with its specific analysis and its decisions to make. When we look at an object, say a car, we need to see it from all angles to get an exact idea of what it is like. We need a 360° view to be sure we know its shape, design, profile and so on. The same is true of a company; to grasp its strategic position we have to observe it, analyze it, from all angles. Each angle will provide a particular kind of information, lead us to certain conclusions, and demand a certain type of decision. Each of these perspectives will lead us to a different analysis and strategic decision. This is what we will develop in the following chapters.

2.6 Policies

Policies are guidelines for action, decision-making criteria to select the right alternative. For example, a company might have the policy of not distributing dividends, or of not accumulating debt, or of giving priority to in-house promotion when filling vacancies.

Policies, therefore, stand on a lower level of importance than strategies. The company stakes its future on its strategy. Strategy is responsible for the company adapting constantly to the changing environment in which it operates (the economy, the industry, the market), and so strategy can never be an unchanging guideline for action – unlike policies, which remain stable for long periods of time.

If a company does not distribute dividends or avoids accumulating debt, usually it will not reconsider these policies for some time, among other reasons because these policies are related to its values (as we already know, all the key concepts are interrelated). If a company does not distribute dividends and avoids accumulating debt, it will usually be because its values are fairly conservative and its risk aversion high. Hence its owners do not want to expose themselves to the danger that may be involved in high debt and prefer to invest their profits in the company. This is another illustration of why values are at the base of the sculpture that we are building with the key concepts.

Policies are guidelines for action that are almost permanent, but not unalterable. A company might have the policies of distributing high dividends and incurring high debt, but in light of a virulent crisis such as the one experienced from 2007 to 2011 it might decide not to distribute the meager profit obtained (if it is among the few companies that had one) and make do with less funding, in view of the restrictions and conditions imposed by the banks.

While it is true that policies are on a lower level of importance than strategies, and that with strategy the future of the firm is undeniably at stake, this does not signify by any means that policies are not important in their own right. They are important because they can stretch or shrink the company's capacities, and can therefore increase or decrease its strategic possibilities. They either limit or extend the company's field of strategic action; they install "fences" that channel it. If a company has the policy of not giving dividends it is increasing its financial capacity, its strategic possibilities. Similarly if it has the policy of accumulating high levels of debt. And the opposite will be the case if its policies are to distribute a high dividend and incur very little debt, thus restricting its capacities.

If we take a look at Figure 2.1, we will see that policies are depicted alongside strategies, occupying less space; this is to convey the idea that they act as decision-making guidelines, although they are less important ones than strategies.

2.7 Concepts and Labels

It must be borne in mind that business policy, the area of knowledge of business strategy, has a degree of subjectivity. It is not an exact science. A number of books can be found in which the authors differ on how to define these key concepts. We even find examples of managers or entrepreneurs who define these key concepts in a way that academically could be classed as wrong – yet they have been extremely successful in business, despite their incorrect definitions.

This leads us to a conclusion that is worth emphasizing. The important thing is the concept. The name we give it is the least of our concerns. Just as in medicine the active ingredient is what cures and not the brand name (it could be called anything; indeed, if two laboratories get the patent they may give it two different names). The same happens with key strategic concepts. The essential thing is the concepts themselves and how they are defined; the names we give them don't matter. The essential thing, the most indispensable thing for a company, is to know what it believes in (values), to be aware of what it does (mission), to set forth what it wants to become in the future (vision), to have this goal in quantified form (objectives), to know how it is going to achieve it (strategy) and to have guidelines for action (policies). If instead of these labels or names it gives them different ones, no problem will ensue – as long as it has a clear perception of these six concepts, no matter what it calls them.

As a result, we may find cases of firms that confuse the name they give to one or other of these concepts, but nevertheless obtain highly positive results. To sum up, the discussion should be about concepts; we should waste no time with debates on the labels attached to these concepts. We must always remember that the key factor is the active ingredient, not the brand name or whether the bottle is green or yellow.

2.8 Beginning and End of the GIB Model

We started this chapter with the statement that defining the company's key strategic concepts is stage zero of a process of strategic thinking; that this process must begin with in-depth knowledge of the current state of the company in these concepts. So, we now have the beginning of the thinking process, and we are also familiarized with its last stage. We know that when the whole process is complete the company will rethink these key concepts (all of them except values, which, as we have discussed, are

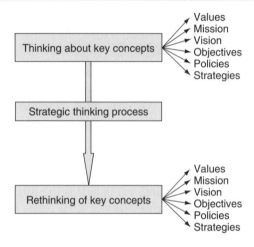

Figure 2.2 Situation at the beginning and the end of the GIB model

intrinsic to its owners and will only change if the identity of the owners changes).

Figure 2.2 presents the first stage of the **GIB** (**G**eneral, **I**ntegrative and **B**asic) model, the strategic thinking model that will be developed in the course of this book. **G**eneral because it structures all the concepts and analyses that really matter when thinking strategically about business. **B**asic because it is fundamental to think about each of these concepts and analyses, although logically some will be more important than others for each company, depending on its industry and its strategy. But what the GIB model seeks to contribute above all is the "**I**" in the middle of its name. Its main aim is to **I**ntegrate the concepts and analyses on which a strategic formulation process is based, to highlight the interrelationship between them.

All the strategic concepts are interrelated; when one changes, this affects the rest. A strategic thinking model is like a living jigsaw puzzle, in constant evolution, with interrelating pieces that constantly change shape and size. This is what the GIB model is intended to show, and it is the main contribution that it is intended to make. Building it chapter by chapter, concept by concept, analysis by analysis, helps us to understand this interrelationship.

In order to build the bridge that will lead us to the current state of the company, the beginning of the thinking process, on our way towards its competitive improvement at the end of the process, we will have to consider its position from a maximum number of perspectives, from as many angles as possible, trying to relate them to each other and so piece together an overall, real and effective view. As we have already mentioned, if we look at any object – for example, a house in the country – from one position, we will have one angle of vision, one perspective, which will give us one piece of information. If we look at it from another position our conclusions might be different. And if we had a third perspective maybe we would change our mind yet again.

Taking the example of the house in the country, if we look at it from the front we might think it meets our needs as regards surroundings, size, state of repair and so on. But we can only be sure about some of these characteristics if we take a good look inside. And if we could see the back of the house we might find that it has a well-kept garden and a modern swimming pool, which would increase our interest. However, if in the end we managed to get a bird's eye view revealing that the roof is in a deplorable state and can only be fixed by spending a large amount of money, our opinion would change radically. Only the entire range of perspectives provides a real, complete and integral view of what the house is like and what features can be expected from it.

The same happens with a company. In order to analyze its state we need the maximum number of different views, as many perspectives as possible. Translated into strategic language, this means the maximum possible number of analyses and concepts, both internally, within the firm itself, and externally, since as we mentioned earlier, in the strategic game it is basic to adapt to the economic, political and social situation, to customers' needs, and to do so better than one's competitors, all of which are external aspects.

This is the essence of the strategic formulation process: to analyze both the environment and the inner workings of the company. And in this analysis the GIB model goes all the way, breaking down each of these analyses into as many perspectives as possible, because it takes into account the fact that the deeper the analysis, the better the information, and therefore the smaller the risk of making the wrong decision. Unfortunately it is impossible to eliminate risk from strategic decisions. They involve risk by definition. Making strategic decisions means making a series of hypotheses about the future situation of the environment (the economy, the industry, the market) that can by no means be guaranteed. However, by increasing the depth of the analyses of the environment and the inside of the company, this risk diminishes. With this perspective we can take a small step further, describing the GIB model by introducing both of these analyses as a way of bonding the beginning and the end of the thinking process, as shown in Figure 2.3 below.

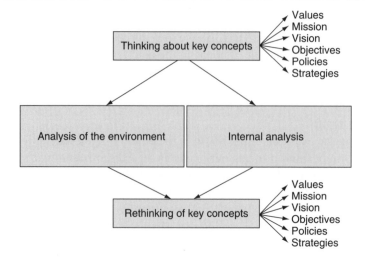

Figure 2.3 Situation at the beginning and the end of the GIB model: the formulation process as nexus

2.9 Questions for Reflection

I. What are the values of your company?

II. Are they shared by the management team?

III. What is the mission of your company?

IV. How would you define its mission, expressed as a business concept?

    a. What needs does it satisfy?

    b. For whom? (Market segments)

    c. How? (Technology or know-how)

V. What is the vision of your organization?

VI. What objectives does it have as a business?

VII. What policies does your company have?

VIII. What main strategic lines does it follow?

IX. Do you think these key concepts are consistent with each other in your firm?

X. What could its mission or business concept be in the future?

XI. Do you think in the future it might be feasible to define an innovative mission or business concept, aside from the conventionalisms of the industry?

CHAPTER 3

Competitive Advantage and Strategy

In 1759 Arthur Guinness, at the age of 34, signed a lease for 9000 years (that's not a typing error, it was a nine-thousand year lease) on an old disused and poorly equipped brewery at St. James's Gate in Dublin.[1] The deal was closed with the payment of £100 plus an annual rent of a further £45. This rent included decisive rights over the water supply, of vital importance for brewing. The brewery covered 4 acres (1.62 hectares).

Guinness has maintained a competitive advantage for over 250 years, not exactly the same one for these two and a half centuries, but with a competitive advantage to this day, and one that now manages to get more than 10 million pints consumed daily throughout 150 countries.[2] All companies, if they are in a particular industry, have a competitive advantage. They could not live without it (beyond the time needed to use up all its resources). Therefore, having and maintaining – because it has to be sustainable in the long term – a competitive advantage is an indispensable condition. This is one of the main responsibilities of company management.

3.1 Competitive Advantage

A competitive advantage must be sustainable; it must be protected in some way. If it is not, the advantage will immediately be copied and then it will cease to be an advantage. For example, imagine a bank that creates a new financial product. If it is successful it will easily be copied by its competitors, so the superiority provided by this product will be fleeting. In the course of this book we will describe various ways of protecting a competitive advantage, although this always depends on the type of advantage concerned.

Competitive advantage has the added difficulty of not being an absolute concept but a relative one: it is not a matter of being good, but of being better. There is a big difference; it is hard enough to be good or very good, but it is even harder to be better. One company is better by comparison, and achieving this involves the difficulty of constantly competing with other companies that seek that same advantage.

It is true that there may be cases in which several competitors coexist using the same strategy. These competitors will usually be targeting a sufficiently broad market for them all to have enough customers to survive. But even in such cases, the competition puts the advantage to the test daily. Therefore competitive advantage has an expiry date. It is necessary to be constantly on the lookout for this potential end of cycle, and to be sure that when it comes there will be a new advantage to take its place. As we mentioned earlier, Guinness is over 250 years old, but its current competitive advantage is a lot younger than that. This Irish company has had to reformulate its strategy time and time again over the last two and a half centuries in order to reach such a respectable age in such an appreciably youthful state of health.

As we will see, there are many kinds of competitive advantage. Michael Porter provided a very good definition of the three main routes that can lead a company to this enviable position. He called them the three generic strategies;[3] they are like the three major motorways that can lead to business success – unless we have an accident along the way. But we need to bear in mind that at the end of these motorways there are (as we will see) a series of trunk roads, each of which lead to a large number of main roads, and so on until in the end we find ourselves driving down country lanes. So in fact there are many types of competitive advantage, not just three. In short, the three generic strategies are merely the way into strategy; after this, we have to carry on dissecting a company's strategy in order to be capable of understanding it perfectly.

In fact, we can simplify competitive advantage still further, since if we look at Figure 3.1 we will see that, taking synthesis to an extreme, there are two main ways of obtaining competitive advantage: exclusivity (differentiation) and cost. This is so because the third generic strategy appears when we think where this advantage is applied, whether in the whole industry or only part of it.

3.2 Differentiation Strategy

The first type of competitive advantage is the sort gained by a company when it has a characteristic that is better than its competitors' and when this is perceived and appreciated by the customer. This company obtains

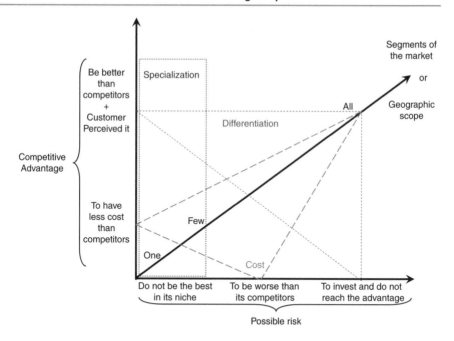

Figure 3.1   Competitive advantage, generic strategies and their possible
risks

exclusivity, and this is the sort of advantage that leads to the strategy of
differentiation, as depicted in Figure 3.1. Consequently, in order for a company to possess differentiation, it must fulfil both requirements: it must
stand out from its competitors in some key aspect or aspects for its industry
(nearly always a combination of factors), and this must be appreciated and
perceived by its customers.

It is impossible to provide a definitive list of strategic roads to gaining differentiation – first, because it would be a very long one, and second,
because it wouldn't be correct: there are too many ways of achieving differentiation, some of them applicable only to certain industries, and above all,
every day companies try to find new ways (and some of them succeed), so
the list would be constantly expanding. However, what we can offer is a few
examples of the most usual ways of obtaining this competitive advantage:

■   **Quality.** If we think of the best brands in any industry (e.g. cosmet-
    ics, fashion, cars, electronics) we associate their products with quality,
    together with other factors described below, since as we have already
    mentioned, differentiation is usually achieved through a combination of
    factors.

- **Innovation.** Companies like Apple are constantly thinking how to modify different characteristics of their products, or even better, generate new products before their competitors do so. They always want to be the first to launch new products onto the market. The iPhone and the iPad were magnificent examples of innovation; no one had ever seen products like them before. The spirit (and the strategy) of Apple is to be constantly ahead of its time. We should also mention Google, capable of creating Google Earth by combining satellite images, maps and the capacity of its search engine, thus making it possible to view any place on the planet in detail.

- **Design.** A key ingredient in the world of fashion, cars, electronics and others. Here too, Apple stands out. Its design is crucial in achieving the youthful, modern, fun brand image it seeks to convey. Design has become such an important aspect in so many industries that in some it constitutes a minimum requirement: without design one cannot be competitive. Later on we will go into greater detail about this dual-level phenomenon that can be found in a strategic approach such as design, whereby a minimum level can be required to be in the running at all, and a higher level to break away from the pack.

- **Technology or know-how.** A key factor in many industries, technology usually translates as the possibility of attaining other characteristics described here (such as quality and design). We should bear in mind, and we will emphasize below, that the sorts of capabilities that are going to provide competitive advantage are usually intangible ones.

- **Service.** A key way to differentiate in many industries, especially when the rest of the variables are equal. For example, the financial products of the various banks are increasingly homogeneous, so the consumer increasingly takes into account the service quality provided. If the authorized dealers of a particular car maker in a city all offer exactly the same products, what will the customer's choice be based on?

- **Channel.** A form of distribution. Companies that target the luxury segment of industries such as fashion, cosmetics and watches differentiate themselves by selling their products very exclusively, making them available only in a few select shops.

- **Brand image.** Closely linked to one of the points that we have already singled out as essential to achieving differentiation. Not only is it necessary to be exclusive, to have a better key characteristic than the competition; this aspect must also be perceived by the customer – the company must be able to communicate it. Before brand image comes brand awareness – getting the consumer to know that the brand exists. The purpose of brand image is for the company to be perceived as better than its competitors in those factors in which it wants to stand out, in which it wants to position itself. As advertising copywriter Toni Segarra says: "If products and brands were really as different as they're often made out to be, we would be out of a job. Or our job would be much simpler."[4]

In short, if a company is better than the rest, but is not perceived as such by its customers, it will not succeed in differentiating itself, and therefore it will be unable to gain a competitive advantage. Hence the great importance of marketing and all its forms of communication for a company, since it is vital not only to know what customers want and value (likewise the responsibility of the marketing department) but also to know how to tell them so they can perceive it. In fact, the opposite could also happen. A company could be perceived as the best in a particular area (such as service, design, quality) but not actually be the best in that aspect. In this case, this company would get most of the customers, although it would have serious trouble in future continuing to convince those customers that it is the best when this is not true.

The differentiation strategy usually involves a risk for the company, because the fact of achieving that competitive advantage (quality, technology, brand, service, design, innovation) is generally going to require investment, which may or may not succeed in achieving the desired differentiation. If the company makes the investment and fails to achieve the advantage, it has simply incurred an additional cost. For example, it might invest in R&D in an attempt to achieve a new technology, or in operations to improve quality, or in marketing to increase awareness or improve the brand's positioning, but these investments might not enable the firm to improve its technology, quality or brand as intended.

Logically, if the investment is successful the company will usually raise the price of its product or service, as it has customers that are going to appreciate the improvement. Someone who buys an Audi or a Mercedes is willing to pay more than they would for the same model made by other manufacturers, simply because the Audi rings or the Mercedes star (the positioning of these brands) convey better technology, quality and design. This price rise has to cover the investment made by the differentiated company, as a result of which its margin will increase. However, management can always lower the price by giving priority to greater turnover (increased sales) when choosing how to maximize the return on the investment made in order to differentiate itself.

3.3 Cost Leadership Strategy

Not all companies want to differentiate themselves, among other reasons because not all customers want, value or are able to pay for that differentiation. Within this group of companies that do not seek to differentiate themselves, the strategy is to be on the same level as (not worse than!) the rest, but with lower costs. The competitive advantage is low cost, and the generic strategy is known as cost leadership.

It is important to clarify that the competitive advantage is never low price. Price comes later; it is a strategic decision made once the cost advantage has been achieved. Any company can decide to apply low prices, but only the cost leader (the company with the lowest costs in its industry) can maintain them in the long run. However, the company with the lowest costs may decide to apply prices that are not so low, because that larger margin might be fundamental for reinforcing its advantage. In short, having the lowest costs in an industry does not force a company to set low prices. This is one of the advantages of this strategy: it is the only company in its industry that can decide its lower price limit in the long term.

There are several sources of low costs:

- **Low costs due to structural factors.** This is the best source of low costs, as it involves a long-term advantage and company ownership (as we will see, the other cost sources do not meet these premises). This category includes **economies of scale**. In these, unit costs decrease with increasing company size. Economies of scale can occur in all the activities of a company (e.g. R&D, operations, logistics, marketing). For example, Coca-Cola is the soft drinks firm that spends most on advertising. However, in its industry it is one of the companies with the smallest advertising effort per unit sold, once its huge advertising budget is divided by the much larger number of units sold.

  When a decrease in unit cost is due to a gradual accumulation, this is the **learning curve**. In this case, the company does not have lower costs because it is very large (economies of scale) but because of having been in the industry for many years, having learnt things over those years, and being more efficient. The learning curve is one of the components of experience; any worker does his job better as he practices it, and this enhanced know-how is consolidated in the company.

  Specialization or division of labour also increases the efficiency of an operation, as do **standardization**, product or machine **redesign**, process **innovation**, and **new materials**, all of which are factors that improve as the company acquires experience. The Boston Consulting Group (BCG) explained years ago how the success of Japanese corporations such as Honda in the motorcycle industry was due to the reduction in costs provided by the experience curve; we would find examples in all industries. Having a patented **technology of one own** can be another cause of structurally low costs, as can better **plant design**. And we have already seen at the beginning of this chapter how **sharing activities** in the case of diversified companies can be another source of lower costs.

■ **Low cost due to execution.** The second type of cost source is that derived from execution. These costs are less beneficial than the structural sort, as they do not belong to the company, and they are not so long-term, since they depend on people. Having a better management team, or better staff in general, or managers who are good at negotiating with suppliers or customers, or who have a good relationship with them and the rest of the stakeholders or other institutions directly linked to the company (banks, government bodies), can all give a company a cost advantage. However, when these managers or staff leave the company, the advantage will disappear. This is why, when one company takes over another, one of the conditions for the purchase is sometimes that the key managers of the company that is taken over must remain in it.

■ **Low cost due to external causes.** Finally, there is no cost source worse than one based on causes that are external to the company. If a company benefits from lower costs due to a favorable exchange rate or the temporary price of a commodity (oil or other raw materials) it will never be able to dominate that advantage, as it does not belong to the company. Just as at one particular moment the exchange rate or the price of a key raw material is favorable to the company, subsequently they may be extremely harmful.

Low-cost strategies. It is undeniable that the strategy of low costs, although it is not necessarily linked to that of low prices, has been responsible for the unstoppable and widespread eruption of low-cost strategies in most industries, clearly resulting in competition based on low prices. For it to be possible to buy an airline ticket to any European city for €20, €10 or even €0 plus taxes and fees, or to furnish practically a whole house for little more €1000, or to buy what a so-called own-brand product between 18 percent and 42 percent cheaper than one that is almost identical,[5] the companies that sell them have had to stick slavishly to a low-cost strategy.

These strategies are based on the cost sources mentioned above, but often also on the idea of the customer doing part of the work that used to be done by the company. In an excellent short article, Ramón Muñoz described this phenomenon with a wry sense of humor: "The customer is no longer boss; quite the opposite, he's a grafter. We serve ourselves with petrol, we weigh our own fruit at the supermarket, we put our rubbish into 27 different coloured containers, we assemble our own Ikea furniture, we install our own broadband . . . . And to add insult to injury, we pay for it all! Soon the funeral directors will be putting up notices in the hospitals saying 'Just before you die, remember to get in your coffin and please close the lid gently.' "[6]

3.4 Specialization Strategy

We said at the beginning of this chapter that competitive advantage can be divided into two approaches: differentiation (customer-perceived exclusivity) and cost leadership (low-cost position). However, we also mentioned that there are three generic strategies or main strategic directions that a company can follow, as depicted in Figure 3.1.

The most important feature of the third of these generic strategies is not whether the company achieves its competitive advantage via differentiation or costs; rather, the most significant aspect is its strategic objective. The strategy of specialization does not target the whole industry but only part of it. This part can be either **geographical** (regarding the industry as a territorial area) or by **needs** (regarding it as a set of needs).

As we mentioned earlier, there are many definitions of strategy, and one of them states that strategy is a process of negation, of accepting that the company cannot do everything. This characteristic is brought to the fore in the specialization strategy. A company that specializes targets only part of its industry and renounces the rest; in some cases this part that it deliberately decides not to target can be very large.

Newspapers provide a good example for observing this strategy. There are national newspapers in which we find all sorts of news (international, national, politics, comment, sports, business). But there are also local papers covering a smaller territorial area, and then there are the sports and financial press. The advantage sought by this second group (both local newspapers and the sports and financial press) lies clearly in their specialization. If they have renounced a large part of their industry it is to meet the needs of the niche that they target better than other companies. The local press is a case of geographical specialization, whereas sports and financial newspapers are examples of specialization by needs, by market segments.

The strategic objective of a local newspaper is to get people who value and want more and better news about their city or area to choose it instead of a national paper. And it tries to get readers to opt for it because, although they will find better international, national, sports and financial news and comment in a national paper, they are going to find less specific information about their city and area, which is precisely what the reader they target is looking for. In a national paper local news tends to be squeezed into just a few pages, whereas the whole of the local paper, each and every page of it, is written from this angle.

Similarly, a sports paper seeks to get readers who want to know all about sports to buy it instead of a general newspaper in which they will find only a few pages on sports. As a publication specializing in sports, this type of paper devotes all its pages to this topic.

Therefore, the advantage of this approach must derive from specialization itself, from concentrating on one part of the industry, knowing much more about that niche and thus meeting those customers' needs much better than companies that target the whole industry.

While this is the main reason for specialization, we cannot forget that there might also be reasons of cost. If a company operates only in one geographical area, or in one market segment, its structure (staff, facilities, machinery) will be smaller than that of companies operating in the whole industry. But we should not forget that in some industries these lower structural costs may be insufficient as a competitive advantage, or simply untrue at a unit level due to economies of scale and other synergies provided by larger size.

3.5 Stuck in the Middle

It is not impossible to achieve all three generic strategies at once, but it is very difficult. In fact it is very human to want to do so; we all want to be the best, at a low cost, and to make everybody happy, but the attempt clearly involves risk. This is due to the fact that the three strategies are interrelated, as we see in Figure 3.2. This figure depicts the case of a company with low costs that also wants to achieve differentiation. There is a danger that in the attempt to achieve this differentiation its costs will rise (precisely because of the cost incurred by trying to achieve differentiation). The company runs the risk of failing to achieve the desired differentiation and at the same time losing the low-cost position it had.

Michael Porter coined the term 'stuck in the middle' to describe those companies that, by attempting to achieve all the generic strategies, actually fulfil none of them. Companies that decide to differentiate themselves beat them at that strategic game, those that want to be cost leaders beat them at theirs, and in turn those that specialize in their targeted market niches beat them on that count. Wanting it all, wanting to be the best at low cost and

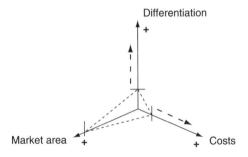

Figure 3.2 Interrelation between the three generic strategies

serving all sorts of customers satisfactorily, is a desire that is as human as it is difficult to achieve.

However, it is not impossible. Many years ago now, IBM dominated its market completely and enjoyed both differentiation and cost leadership. However, when the rules of the industry changed its advantages crumbled rapidly. One way of achieving all the generic strategies is for Figure 3.2 not to be true, to be able to achieve differentiation without costs rising (or without them rising very significantly). This can happen when the differentiation is based on an idea. How much does an idea cost? We will all agree that it requires effort to have a good idea, but the monetary cost is zero.

An example of this would be Priceline.com, a business based on an idea patented by its inventor, Jay Walker. On the face of it, it did not seem a particularly extraordinary idea: it was simply a reverse auction (one in which the customer sets the price) of such everyday products as airline tickets, hotel rooms, hire cars and so on. Yet this concept led Priceline.com to be valued at $20,000 million when it was floated on the stock exchange in 1999 (and more than this figure at the beginning of 2011). This simple but appreciated (by his customers) idea enabled Walker to differentiate his business very significantly at a very low cost, thus achieving both advantages, and in his case patenting the idea. If he had not done so, his brilliant idea would have been copied as soon as it proved successful and the value of Priceline.com would have been very close to zero.

3.6 Making the Generic Strategies Specific

The generic strategies describe the three main strategic channels. In some cases it is obvious which strategy a company follows. Audi, Mercedes and BMW follow the differentiation strategy, while the Indian company Tata follows the cost strategy by producing extremely cheap cars, and Ferrari specializes in luxury sports cars. These cases are extremely clear.

However, with other companies, we are unable to say for sure which of the three strategic roads they follow. This would be the case of Benetton or Zara clothes or Swatch watches. They have some differentiation aspects, but they also have cost components, and they are hardly 'stuck in the middle'. This shows that generic strategies are a very good introduction to strategy; they clarify the main strategic lines very well, but they are too generic, as their name indicates. Hence the need to penetrate further into competitive advantage, to have more tools for analysis within our grasp. We will go into further detail about competitive advantage when we analyze the industry.

Figure 3.3 shows us the addition of the generic strategies to the GIB model. Obviously they appear in the decisions section, since one of the imperatives of the thinking process is that the company must have competitive advantage.

However, later on the generic strategies will disappear from the GIB model, because as we have explained, they are too generic. They will be replaced by another strategic concept that will describe competitive advantage much more precisely.

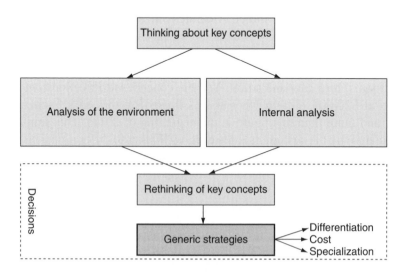

Figure 3.3 Addition of the generic strategies to the GIB model

3.7 Questions for Reflection

Bearing in mind what we have discussed so far:

I.   What competitive advantage/s do you think your company has? Why do your customers buy from you?

II. Do you think your company clearly follows one of the three generic strategies? If so, which one?

III. Does your company's strategy have some differentiation component?

IV. Does it have some cost element?

V.   Does it have some specialization characteristic?

VI. Could it fall into the (very serious) error of being 'stuck in the middle'?

CHAPTER 4

Macro Environment

The world changed in 2007. It changed for the worse, and the trouble deepened between 2008 and 2010. An intense crisis of financial origin caused many economic and social variables to deteriorate. The growth that had existed worldwide in previous years and had been vigorous in many developing and some Western countries, turned into a global recession with a significantly negative gross domestic product (GDP) in many countries. Unemployment shot up to alarming levels. This, together with the concern felt by the employed that they too might lose their jobs, exacerbated consumers' fear of an uncertain future. Like a dog chasing its tail, this resulted in a drop in consumption and caused further economic deterioration and more unemployment. Funding from banks dried up (remember that the origin of the crisis was financial), leaving many companies with extremely serious problems since they were unable to renew their credits, which choked their day-to-day running.

4.1 Macro Environment and Industry Environment

All these variables affected companies greatly, in some cases to the extent that they disappeared. They were all environmental variables; to be more exact, macro-environmental ones. Any factor that is external to the company forms part of its environment. But there are two very different types of environment. There is an environment that is very close to the company, that of its industry, and then there is a more distant environment, the macro environment, to which all the examples described above at the beginning of this chapter belong.

The industry environment is made up solely of those companies that belong to the industry analyzed in each case, whereas all the companies in the geographical area under consideration (a country, a region or the world), no matter what industry they operate in, belong to the macro environment. Therefore, the industry environment is much closer to the company, and as a result is much more restricted as regards its components. The macro environment is much broader.

One fundamental difference is that although we find variables that have a profound influence on the development of a company in both types of environment, in the industry environment the company can influence the variables. This is hardly ever possible in the macro environment. If we think of the examples given at the beginning of this chapter, it will be clear that no company can exert a significant influence on those factors (GDP, funding, unemployment). However, as we will see presently, a company does influence the variables of its industry.

This is because the company is one of the actors in the play as regards its industry. It is one of the teams in the league, and it will influence it, to a greater or lesser extent depending on its size and capability. Therefore, within the industry a company influences and is influenced. It is quite different from the macro environment, in which the company's capacity to influence its surroundings is almost nonexistent, as we will see. The macro environment is like the weather for a football team. The trainer can do nothing to make the sun shine or the rain pour, but the team is drastically influenced by these meteorological conditions. It's not the same to play on a pitch in perfect conditions as it is to play in a quagmire. A trainer cannot influence the weather, but he must adapt to it, react (change his line-up) according to the conditions. This is the spirit in which the company should face the macro environment.

4.2 PEST Analysis

The macro environment can be broken down into four main parts: the economic, social, political and legal, and technological environments, as shown in Figure 4.1. This figure also draws attention to the differences between the macro environment and the industry environment as regards the capacity the company holds to influence each of them. The political and legal, economic, social and technological environments are known by the acronym PEST, although the natural environment or ecological factors can also be included, thus giving the name PESTEL.

Many of the variables described at the beginning of this chapter, to illustrate how the raging crisis at the end of the first decade of the twenty-first century had such a lethal effect on companies in all industries, were

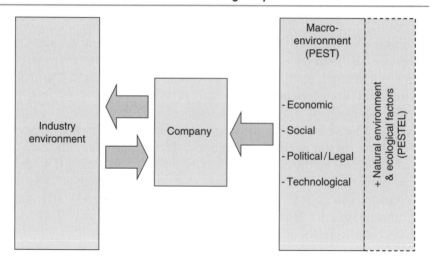

Figure 4.1   The different influences of the macro and the industry environment

economic. The growth (GDP) of a country or an area, unemployment and the ability to obtain funding are all economic factors, as are interest rates, exchange rates, inflation and per capita income. Economic factors are usually present in the day-to-day running of the business, as practically no company can help being related to economic health (GDP and per capita income) or inflation in their area of action. Similarly, very few can escape from being influenced by the situation of the interest rate or the exchange rate, as practically all companies are in debt to some degree and trade with (buy from or sell to) areas that have different currencies.

Continuing with our original example, unemployment can also be considered a social variable, as can the fear of an uncertain future, resulting in lower consumption. Other social variables that can influence companies greatly are the birth rate (if the company targets babies, children or teenagers) and life expectancy (if it targets senior citizens). Other social factors that may affect a company are demography, migratory movements, changes in life style (far-reaching in recent years), income distribution, level of education, industrial conflict (and the strikes that may be associated with it) and the attitude towards work and free time.

Another important change of environment occurs when a new regulation appears in the industry, whether on a local, national or supranational (e.g. European Union) level. This new regulation may come as a "change of pack," a new set of rules to play by. Such changes form part of the political and legal environment, together with any law that might affect the industry, such as labor, environmental or patent legislation, tax policy, tariffs or subsidies.

Lastly, when we refer to the technological environment we mean horizontal technologies, not those restricted to one industry (which we will find in the industry environment). We can think of technologies such as the Internet, cell phones, automation, information systems, robotics or any other technical or scientific discovery that can be applied to an industry. When the Internet and cell phones appeared, the first companies in each industry to discover they could use them to communicate with their customers rapidly and effectively had an advantage over their competitors.

Other variables of the macro environment cannot be attributed to any of the four types of environment described above, but they too must be considered part of it. For example, the climate can be very important for some industries and companies. Tourism, ice creams, textiles and many other industries can be burdened or benefited by climatological factors. Imagine the effect of a very mild winter on clothes manufacturers, or the consequences of a cold, wet summer on ice cream makers and distributors and tourism-related industries.

As we mentioned at the beginning of this section, issues related to the natural environment and ecology, such as awareness of waste treatment, energy consumption and environmental protection, also form part of the macro environment (although the laws derived from this awareness form part of the legal environment).

4.3 Macro Environment and Strategy

Of all the stages in a strategic thinking process, the macro environment is one of the most curious, as its influence on the process, and consequently on company strategy, is as easy to explain as its influences are potentially shattering. As an example of the latter, the deep crisis of 2007–2011 made a great impact – a huge number of companies succumbed to its awful effects, all of them arising from the macro environment. There was hardly a company that escaped its ravages. The devastation that can derive from the macro environment is beyond any doubt. Likewise, on other occasions its effects can be a great blessing.

However, unlike other stages of the strategic thinking process, this very notable effect of the macro environment is easy to explain, and comfortable to monitor – in theory. In fact, it boils down to one key question.

As we know, there are a host of variables in the macro environment, hundreds of economic, social, political and legal, and technological variables. However, from a strategic point of view, a company is only interested in those variables that affect it. And what macro-environmental variables affect a company strategically? The answer is simple (theoretically). The macro-environmental variables that affect a company strategically are those that, when they change, require a change in the company strategy too, an adaptation to that change. The strategy of the company has to be renewed because the changes in these variables have such a great impact on it that the company is unable to avoid adapting to them.

Let us consider the crisis at the end of the first decade of this century. The change of economic cycle, the appearance of a recession (a negative GDP for two quarters or more), caused sales in many markets to drop by often dramatic proportions. At the same time, the drought in the financial market and the drastic cutback in banks' level of lending also drained companies' borrowing power. Consequently, we can say that GDP and borrowing power are macro-environmental variables that affect most companies. When they change, companies have to make changes in their strategy. As a result of the crisis, most (if not all) organizations had to adapt their strategy to the slacker demand (with the exception of a mere handful of industries) and survive on less credit.

So, the key strategic question at this stage of the thinking process is: what macro-environmental variables affect strategy? It is a crucial question, and therefore it is essential to be absolutely clear when answering it. If a change in these macro-environmental factors forces enterprises to rethink their strategy, obviously it is important to know what they are. If they do not, the company will overlook change in the fundamental variables in its macro environment, failing to adjust its strategy to adapt to it, and by the time it feels the effects it will be too late. Remember that strategy is, among other things, the art of being ahead of the effects of changes in the environment, of being able to adapt to it in time.

It is imperative to be very clear when answering the key question of this stage in the thinking process, as the key environmental variables must be monitored almost constantly to avoid the company being surprised by the outcome of their sometimes terrible changes – although of course there will also be times when they will offer incredible opportunities to those firms that detect positive changes before their competitors. Indeed, that alone is more than sufficient reason to do this monitoring.

If a company is properly acquainted with the macro-environmental variables that affect it, it will soon know how they will influence its strategy according to the type of change occurring, and finally it will be able to adapt its strategy and its organization to this new environment.

Here we can make a distinction between different types of macro-environmental variables. Many of the variables we have talked about so far are what we could call "pendulum variables", in the sense that they swing to and fro and if they benefit us one minute they may harm us the next. A pendulum is a good description of the way these variables behave, but a more exact image would be one of a hypothetical pendulum that moves rapidly and irregularly, because of course one characteristic these variables unfortunately do not possess, unlike a real pendulum, is predictability of movement.

Factors such as GDP, the interest rate and the exchange rate move like an unpredictable pendulum. One day they favor us immensely, then suddenly they are pummeling us mercilessly, and in no time at all they are smiling at us again. The changes are continuous and abrupt. Think how violently the last crisis appeared, and how rapidly the GDP plummeted in most countries, since in just a few months vigorous growth was replaced by negative rates. Or take the example of the exchange rate between the euro and the dollar. The euro was first quoted in January 1999, at $1.17. However, by October 2000 (less than two years later) the European single currency had fallen to $0.82 (a 30 percent depreciation). Yet in July 2008 it reached $1.60, an appreciation of almost 100 percent over October 2000!

Turning to interest rates, we see how the European Central Bank (ECB) had fixed rates at 4.25 percent in October 2008, only to lower them to 1 percent in May 2009. In just seven months interest rates were cut to less than a quarter. If we analyze the behavior of the US Federal Reserve it was even more abrupt, since in just under a year it cut rates from 4.25 percent to practically zero; in December 2008 interest rates were fixed at a historical low ranging from 0 to 0.25 percent.

Clearly, then, the behavior of these macro-environmental variables is absolutely pendulum-like, jerking unpredictably up and down.

On the other hand, other macro-environmental variables behave more as trends. Their movements are not abrupt but linear, they are not rapid but very gradual, and rather than unpredictable they are fairly predictable. For example, in Western countries life expectancy is increasing slowly but inexorably, in a linear and predictable fashion. Similarly, the development of the future world powers, emerging countries such as China, India and Brazil, seems to be following this same rising trend. Phenomena such as the digital revolution and global warming could also be included as trends. None of these factors make abrupt, rapid or unpredictable movements. On the contrary, they are linear, slow and predictable. Although they are slow, we do not know exactly what speed they will move at, but we know their direction, we know where they are leading us.

Strategically, these macro-environmental factors should be observed differently. If pendulum variables must be watched practically on a day-to-day basis, constantly, because we don't know when they are going to change radically, trend variables can be monitored from a certain distance, without constant observation.

But this does not mean we should neglect them. If we have the opportunity to operate in markets that serve the elderly, we know the markets will grow. If we start to get competitors in emerging countries, we can be sure that these competitors will get bigger and better all the time. If we have a business related to tourism, for example a relatively low-altitude ski station with winter temperatures only just below zero, we can forecast that in a few years we may have to close the business, since with even a very slightly warmer climate there will no longer be enough snow. None of these opportunities or threats is imminent; they are all long-term trends. But they are there, in the company's environment, advancing slowly but inexorably. Although we do not keep a daily check on them as we do with pendulum variables, we cannot forget about them.

Figure 4.2 depicts the addition of macro-environmental analysis to the GIB model.

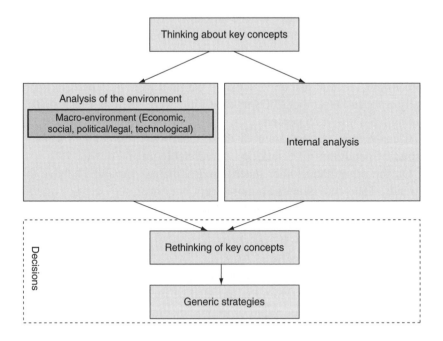

Figure 4.2 Addition of macro-environmental analysis to the GIB model

4.4 Types of Environment

If we want to define a company's environment we can do so on the basis of three different dimensions. One is the number of variables that affect the company, and is known as the complexity of the environment. Another is whether these variables change quickly or slowly: the dynamism of the environment. And finally we can consider whether the changes are predictable or not: the uncertainty of the environment. By combining this environmental complexity, dynamism and uncertainty we get all the various possible types of environment, as shown in Figure 4.3.

Naturally, all these characteristics manifest themselves when we look at the environment as a whole, all the environments we will go on to describe and analyze in this book, and not just the macro environment (the only environment we have described so far). Although there are still a considerable number of environmental perspectives to introduce and analyze, it is desirable to have an idea of what the environment may be like as soon as we start to work our way into it. And it is also desirable, right from the start, to take into account the idea provided by the scenario method.

As we can see in Figure 4.3, with regard to complexity, if a company is affected by only a few variables its environment is simple, and conversely if it is affected by many it will be complex. Dynamism will tell us whether

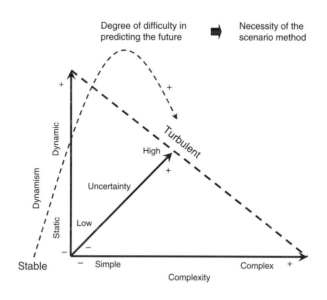

Figure 4.3 The environment's triangle

these variables – be they few or many – change quickly or slowly. If change is gradual the environment will be static, whereas if change is fast it will be dynamic. Lastly, the environment will be low-uncertainty if the changes are predictable and high-uncertainty if they are unpredictable.

Referring to Figure 4.3, we can describe the two extremes. One is a stable environment, characterized by being simple, static and low-uncertainty. In other words, the company is in an environment that is affected by few variables, these variables change slowly, and moreover the changes are predictable. At the other extreme, the environment has the opposite characteristics: it is turbulent, so it is complex, dynamic and high-uncertainty. It is, therefore, an environment in which many variables affect the company, they change very rapidly, and change is unpredictable.

It is not very difficult to imagine what sort of environment surrounds the vast majority of companies in the second decade of the twenty-first century. With extremely few exceptions, we live in a turbulent world. Almost all industries are in this situation. This makes it really much more difficult to think strategically, to prepare for the future, which is what strategy demands of us. In the words of Jack Welch, long-time chairman of General Electric: "When the rate of change inside an institution becomes slower than the rate of change outside, the end is in sight. The only question is when."

Strategy is adaptation to the environment, it is preparing for tomorrow today, by trying to find out what tomorrow might be like. However, if we are fighting against turbulent environments this task is presumably going to be very difficult. We have to think in the long term, yet we find that we cannot foretell the future, we cannot extrapolate from what is happening today.

4.5 Scenarios

The future is unpredictable; nobody knows what it will be like. Even the rating agencies, who make money telling the future, qualifying companies and countries according to their risk, get it wrong sometimes. The crisis of 2007–2011 highlighted the great difficulty of predicting the future of companies and countries, even for the experts.

As the future is unpredictable, risk will never disappear. It will always be closely associated with a company's strategy. However, we can reduce it. In fact, the purpose of the strategic thinking model we are developing (the GIB model), together with each and every one of the analyses and concepts it contains, is to reduce this risk; to diminish it by ensuring that the strategic decision is made on the basis of the most complete information possible and full acceptance of the risk involved. The scenario method works in this direction, by making the management team think about the future, making its members aware of the risks associated with each strategic decision.

The basic idea of the scenario method is that although we cannot foretell the future, as it is impossible to know how things will unfold, perhaps we should think about several futures covering all the various possibilities. In this way we are bound to be looking at the future – in fact, at the full array of possible futures, among which the real future is sure to be there.

Typically, the scenarios could consist of, first, a positive future environment in which all the variables affecting us are assumed to improve; a second scenario which could be described as normal, with a more modest development of these variables; and lastly a negative scenario in which these factors are assumed to deteriorate in the future. Undoubtedly the future is not so black and white, and the scenarios become complicated with the appearance of possible scenarios that are combinations of the above three, with some variables being better and others worse.

Furthermore, scenarios do not always fit into this good-medium-bad framework. They may simply be different scenarios; neither good nor bad, just different. For example, years ago manufacturers of large commercial aircraft considered two types of scenarios. One predicted a future with increased air traffic and hence the need for more aircraft. The other also predicted a future with increased air traffic, but in addition to this it forecast overcrowded air corridors and restrictions on permission to land. This pointed not to a need for more aircraft but rather to a need for larger aircraft. In this case there was no good or bad scenario; they were just two different scenarios. And it seems that Airbus opted for the scenario that forecast larger aircraft by developing the A-380, which can have capacity for up to 850 tourist class seats (or about 550 seats of all classes).

In order to devise a set of scenarios we must follow the stages outlined in Figure 4.4. Before starting, it is important to have a clear idea of the time span for which we want to build the scenarios. The years for which it makes sense to devise scenarios will depend on the industry and the company involved. It might make sense to think about building scenarios for one, three, five, fifteen or even more years, as was the case with the above example of aircraft manufacturers (since the design and development of a new concept of aircraft is a strategic decision that stretches over many years, as well as requiring huge resources).

Once we have decided how many years we are considering, the next stage takes us back to the beginning of this chapter, when we were talking about macro environment and strategy. At that point we said that there is a key strategic question at this stage in the thinking process: what macro-environmental variables affect the company? Out of the wide range of

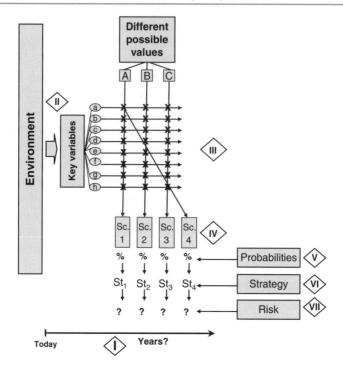

Figure 4.4 Scheme of the scenario method phases

macro-environmental variables, which of them force the company to rethink its strategy when they change?

This is precisely the first key question for building a set of scenarios. The difference is that a set of scenarios is built on the foundation of the whole environment, so this question about the key variables refers to the whole environment, not just the macro environment.

For example, if we think only about the macro environment (the only environment discussed up to now), a company could conclude that its key variables in its own case are: the GDP, the interest rate, the exchange rate, the birth rate and the regulations in force in the area where it operates. This could be because it is a company that would be seriously affected by a recession, it has a high level of debt, it operates in markets that have the dollar and the euro as their currencies, its product is aimed at children, and its industry suffers regulatory changes by the institutions of the areas in which it operates. For this company, considering only the macro environment, its future depends on the development of these variables.

The next stage is about what might happen in the future, in the period of time we have determined, to the key variables selected in the previous stage.

If we continue with the examples given above, we will have to think about what might happen over this period of time to the GDP, the interest rate, the exchange rate and the birth rate, and what possible regulatory changes there might be. As we said earlier, no one can know for sure how these variables will behave in the future, but we can propose ranges of values for each of them. No doubt it is rash to forecast the GDP of an area three years hence, but it is less so to predict that it will lie within a certain range of values that might be wider or narrower depending on the variable concerned. In this way we can have, for example, a minimum value, a maximum one and an intermediate one for each of these variables (GDP, interest rate, exchange rate, birth rate and regulations). And we can also assign a probability to each of these values (remember that the same must be done for the key variables of the rest of the environments which we will analyze in the following chapters).

The last stage is to build the various scenarios on the basis of the values and probabilities obtained in the previous stage. If we select all the values that are negative for the company, we get as a result the negative scenario, and the opposite if we take the positive values. Similarly, we get an intermediate scenario if we choose this type of values. However, as we have already mentioned, there are also scenarios that combine positive and negative values. We should see in each case which scenarios are the most logical. It should be borne in mind that there may be scenarios that are simply different, neither good nor bad. Whatever the scenarios envisaged, they too can be assigned probabilities.

We still don't know the future, but we know possible futures. We have thought about the future and we have been capable of visualizing different possibilities for it. We don't know what the future will be, but we have been there, which is no mean feat.

If we wish to carry on thinking, which is what a thinking process is all about, we can reflect about what needs to be done in each scenario – in other words, if a scenario presented itself, what strategy the company should adopt. In this way, we go deeper into the thinking process. Logically these strategies, which respond to various scenarios, will be fairly different; indeed some will be very different, since if the scenarios differ greatly, the strategies that respond to them must also differ greatly, by definition. If a scenario is negative, the company will adopt a survival strategy, cutting costs and possibly downsizing. Quite the opposite of a strategy that responds to a scenario of growth and abundance.

Further thinking can bring us to consider what would happen if the company decides on one strategy and in the end the scenario is different from what was envisaged. This thinking will provide us with the risk taken by the company by choosing a particular strategy, if it assumes one scenario and a different one is what actually occurs.

Regarding the risk involved in choosing a given strategy in the event of an unforeseen scenario occurring, it is important to take into account that the level of risk varies according to the type of strategy. Some strategies allow a certain amount of back-pedaling, even including the recovery of part of the investment made. But there are other strategies that provide no such middle ground; if you change your mind you lose everything you have invested. For example, any investments made in R&D, in technology, or in marketing with the aim of positioning a brand differently are lost completely with a change of strategy.

There are even some strategies from which there is no going back, as the future of the company is committed to them. This could be the case of the decision by Airbus to develop the A-380. The magnitude of the project (with investment in excess of €10,000 million) was such that outright failure could lead to the disappearance of the company itself. The A-380 suffered a two-year delay due to wiring problems, and this alone caused a drop of 26 percent (€5500 million) in the company's share price and cost the entire top management their jobs. This different risk level associated with each strategy must be taken into account when it is time to make a decision.

On the basis of all these considerations, it is the company that must assume the risk of deciding today in order to prepare for the future, by knowing what may happen in the future (scenarios) and with what probability, what to do in each case (strategy) and the risk involved in each possibility. Risk is always there, but by having access to information about the future, the company can familiarize itself with the risk and usually reduce it.

The fact of having built scenarios should provide the company with more flexibility. The company should rapidly detect changes in its environment as a result of having thought at length about it and its key variables. Furthermore, it should react and respond to those changes promptly, because it has thought about what to do in each case. We could say that scenarios build a memory of the future (when we only possess memory of what we have experienced, of the past).

In fact there is an extremely reduced version of the application of the fundamental idea behind this model. Just asking ourselves "what would I do if X happened?" or "what if ... ?" is a simple but sometimes very powerful way of thinking about scenarios. It projects us into the future, it helps us think out and develop future alternatives, and it stimulates new ideas and thoughts about possible new options for the future.

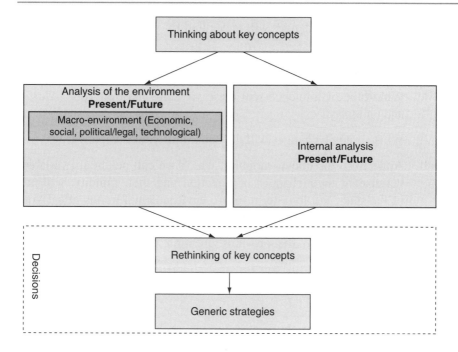

Figure 4.5 Addition of the twofold analysis, present and future, in both environment and internal analysis, to the GIB model

In short, scenarios are not a tool for telling the future but a method that serves to understand trends, to help define problems, and to prepare managers' minds to face them.

In the GIB model (see Figure 4.5), this permanent need to think about the future that is conveyed by the scenario model translates as a twofold analysis of both the environment and the inner workings of the company, in each of the perspectives, each of the analyses, that are going to appear: an analysis of the present, accurate but insufficient, and an analysis of the future, essential but unpredictable.

4.6 Questions for Reflection

I. What macro-environmental (economic, social, political, legal, technological) variables affect your company?

II. What type of influence do these variables have on your industry and company?

III.   What strategic changes will they entail for your company?

IV.   What macro-environmental variables might affect your organization in the future?

V.   What type of influence will these variables have on your industry and company?

VI.   What strategic changes will they entail for your company?

VII.   Apart from the above variables, which we call pendulum variables because of their changes of direction and their rapidity, will any of the mid- and long-term macro-environmental trends affect your industry or company? Which ones?

VIII.   If the answer to the previous question was yes, what strategic decisions do they entail?

IX.   Have you ever used the scenario method or simply the idea, the reasoning behind it?

X.   Do you think it might be useful to you in the future?

CHAPTER 5

Industry Analysis (1): Macro

Undoubtedly it is not the same to be in the telecommunications, airline or drinks industry. Among other things, they differ considerably with regard to competitive structure, types of companies and profitability.

Equally, there is no denying that it is not the same to be, on the one hand, Microsoft, Coca-Cola or Exxon Mobil or, on the other, a local micro-enterprise in one of those same industries. Their strategies, competitive positions and profitability are again quite different.

Because of these differences, an industry needs to be studied. And because the reasons set forth in the above two paragraphs are different, an industry needs to be analyzed on two levels. The first paragraph is about the difference between industries. It is not the same to belong to one or the other; each industry has a different set of characteristics, and this causes each of them to have a different profitability. As it is not the same to be one type of company or another; each company has its own peculiarities that bring it to compete in its own way, and this in turn results in a different profitability for each company.

In short, if we think of industries, we find differences between them; each has its own particular characteristics and, therefore, profitability. And similarly we find differences between companies in the same industry, each again with its own special features and hence its own way of competing and profitability.

5.1 Two Levels of Analysis: Macro and Micro

So the industry is to be analyzed on two levels. The macro level studies the industry overall. It aims to provide a clear picture of the structure of the industry, its appeal, what profit it obtains and especially how it obtains this profit, what reasons account for it. These reasons will enable us to think about the future trend of this profit. This initial industry analysis is general, macro; we are thinking about the whole industry, not the specific case of each of its companies.

This macro industry analysis should answer the question why some industries are more attractive – more profitable – than others. Why, for example, are the pharmaceutical, soft drinks and cosmetics industries usually quite profitable? Why have other industries such as airlines and newspapers come off worse than others in profitability terms at the end of the first decade of the twenty-first century? Why did the economic crisis of 2007–2011 affect the profitability of some industries more than that of others? All these questions should find an answer in this first level of industry analysis.

Figure 5.1 shows in a generic way the relationship between different industries and their profitability.

For example, according to Fortune 500 the most profitable industries in 2007 were network and other communications equipment (with profits

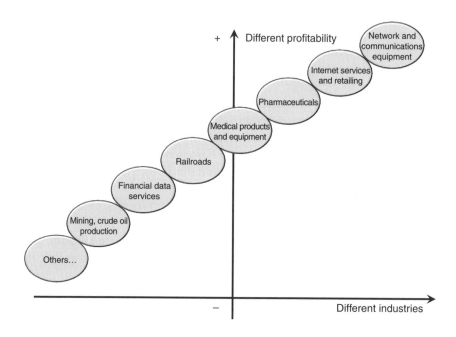

Figure 5.1 Industry and profitability relation (a example from 2007)
Source: Fortune 500, May 5, 2008.

of 20.4 percent on sales), Internet services and retailing (19.4 percent) and pharmaceuticals (19.3 percent). In contrast, the least profitable industries were entertainment (-10 percent), real estate (-13.4 percent) and airlines (-13.5 percent).

Year by year we will find differences in the profits of each industry. We will always need industry analysis to understand the reasons for this varying profitability and, equally important, to be able to think about how it will develop in the future.

The second level of industry analysis is much more micro. Unlike the first level, it is concerned with companies (in the first level we addressed the industry as a whole, not the companies that comprise it). This level aims to show what the industry's companies are like, how they compete, what competitive position they have, what profits they obtain as a result, and what reasons explain this return. It also seeks to predict the trend of this profit.

This second level should answer the question why some companies are more profitable than others in the same industry. Why do Microsoft, Walmart, Johnson & Johnson and Procter & Gamble dominate their industries? Why have companies like Google and Apple developed so positively? In all industries, be they more profitable or less so, there are companies that make big profits, companies that break even, and companies that make a loss. Similarly, some companies show magnificent trends, while others melt in competitive terms like an ice cream in the desert. The aim of this micro industry analysis is to clarify the reasons for these different results and trends.

To sum up, there are two different yet complementary levels of industry analysis, one macro and one micro. In this chapter we will develop and explore the former, and in the next chapter we will address the latter.

5.2 Industry Definitions: Strategic and Analytical

However, before going into these two analyses a company has to think and reach conclusions about two important issues regarding the industry. One is to actually define the industry in which the company operates; this is a strategically crucial aspect. The other is to decide exactly what industry it wants to analyze.

Before performing the industry analysis, a company must be quite clear about what industry it operates in. This is a fundamental and absolutely strategic decision, and we must never start analyzing an industry without facing it. The definition of the industry is one of the most important strategic decisions that a company has to make. It is far-reaching because when we define a company's industry we are defining who its customers, competitors and suppliers are. Therefore, we are defining who the company targets, what needs we want to satisfy, and how we are going to conduct this activity.

In fact, a change in the industry definition implies a change in the company's mission. It means a change in one of its key concepts. If a company changes the definition of its industry it will be in a different business, it will be engaged in a different activity. When we described a company's mission we said that it was like its competitive framework. If it changes, the company will have a different framework and everything will be different within it, not only with regard to the industry (competitors or suppliers) but also regarding the market (customers).

The definition of the industry is essential because it is subjective: there are usually several possibilities. Consequently, the definition depends on the company; it can never be taken for granted. Each company decides where to compete, who its customers are, what needs it wants to satisfy, and how it will do so. An industry can be defined in many ways, some broader and some narrower. It is not the same to be in the food industry as it is to be in the restaurant industry or catering. Each of these definitions specifies more exactly, narrows down the business in which one is involved. As Figure 5.2 tells us, it is not the same to be in the energy drinks industry as it is to be in the soft drinks, non-alcoholic beverages or beverages industry. In each case the industry definition is broader. All these definitions are totally correct, but they are totally different strategically. It is up to the company to decide where it really stands, what it does.

Once a company is clear about which industry it belongs to, it has to think which industry it wants to analyze. It is not the same to analyse catering as to analyze the restaurant industry or the food industry. It is not the same to analyze energy drinks, soft drinks, non-alcoholic beverages or beverages. Each of these possibilities will yield completely different results, as its suppliers, competitors, customers and so on are totally different. We must bear in mind that the broader the definition of the industry we are analyzing, the wider the vision it affords, but at the same time this analysis will be less precise (due to the ever larger number of players involved in each successive industry).

Usually a company will at least analyze the industry that it has defined as its own. However, we might find that the industry under analysis does not coincide with the one that is defined strategically. For example, a company might want to analyze a defined industry that is broader than its own. This could be the case of a company that is quite clear that the strategic definition of its industry is fruit juice concentrate, because it is aware that its

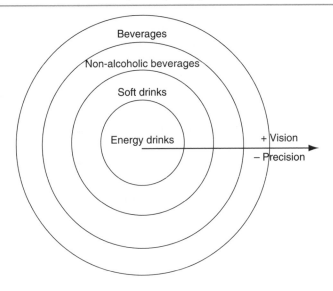

Figure 5.2 Example of different possible definitions of an industry

current capacities provide no margin for any other activities (regardless of whether the company has a vision that might involve extending this industry definition in the future). However, this company might decide to analyze the soft drinks industry; this way it will have a better strategic perspective of what is happening in its industry, as most of its competitors are not limited to making fruit juice concentrate and also have other products in the soft drinks industry. By broadening the industry under analysis it will have greater strategic vision, as we mentioned earlier, but also greater difficulty in the analysis, because of the danger of less precision, as we also mentioned earlier and emphasized in Figure 5.2.

Hence it is necessary to consider both issues: the strategic issue of what industry the company belongs to, and the analytical issue of what industry we wish to analyze.

Logically, both questions have a geographical dimension. The strategic definition must include a geographical area of action, and equally the industry we are analyzing has its geographical limits.

In common with all the other strategic tools and perspectives that we will consider, the industry analysis is dynamic, changing from day to day. Like any analysis, the industry analysis is a snapshot: it reflects the instant it was taken. A moment later, the components of the snapshot have moved. So the industry analysis, like any analysis, is only valid for the moment at which it was performed.

If we add to this the fact that we are engaged in strategic thinking, that we are preparing a company to face the future, we will conclude that, just as we deduced with the scenario method, we have to take two snapshots, two analyses. A present analysis, in this case the snapshot of the industry today, which will be entirely reliable. And then an analysis of the future, of the industry within the time period we are thinking about, which will be less reliable but more interesting than the first when making strategic decisions.

This dichotomy between present and future analyses, reliable but insufficient in the case of the present analysis, unreliable but crucial in the case of the future analysis, will recur in the rest of the analyses we make.

5.3 Industry Analysis (I): Macro

Why does each industry have a different profitability? How can we analyze the causes of an industry's present profitability? How can we study its future trend? Michael Porter provided the answer to these questions many years ago when he first made known his five competitive forces model.[1]

To be exact, these forces are: rivalry, the threat of new competitors, the threat of substitutes, the bargaining power of suppliers, and the bargaining power of customers.

The idea behind this tool is, as shown in Figure 5.3, that each of these five forces struggles to undermine the profitability of the industry. We will all agree that the more rivalry there is in an industry the less profitable it will be. Imagine an industry without rivalry; its profits are bound to be high. However, this high margin will attract other companies wanting to enter the industry. This is where the second force comes in: the threat of new entries. If access to the industry is easy, new competitors will join it until the profitability of the industry is the same as that offered by the financial system for a risk-free investment. Whether or not these new competitors are able to gain entry depends on the entry barriers for the industry.

If we assume that the industry has very high barriers – better still, watertight ones – it will continue to offer the same high profits afforded by its lack of rivalry. However, if this industry has substitutes (the third force) it will never reach a very high profitability because its customers will have an alternative to the industry's products or services. We should remember that a substitute is a product or service from a different industry that meets the same needs as the product or service provided by the industry concerned.

If this hypothetical industry passes the substitutes test (i.e. if it has none) it will continue to yield incredible profits due to the combination

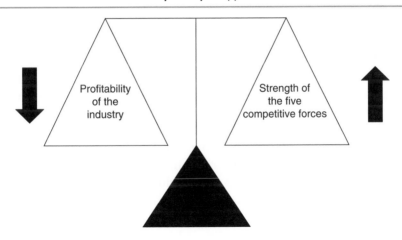

Figure 5.3 The industry' profitability and the five competitive forces

of this absence of substitutes with its lack of rivalry and watertight entry barriers. However, all industries have two leading actors who always feature alongside them on the billboards due to the demands of the screenplay of the business world: all industries have suppliers and customers. What do an industry's suppliers aspire to? To sell their products or services at the highest possible price (or lower the standard and retain the same price). And what do an industry's customers aspire to? To buy its products or services at the lowest possible price (or raise the standard and retain the same price). Translating this to the language of the strategic perspective we are adopting at the moment, what both suppliers and customers aspire to is to corner as much as they can of the industry's profits. They want most of the profit generated in the industry to belong to them. Whether or not they succeed will depend on their bargaining power. For this reason, the bargaining power of suppliers and customers is the fourth and the fifth force.[2]

Only if our hypothetical industry had great bargaining power over its suppliers and customers, in combination with the abovementioned lack of substitutes and rivalry and watertight entry barriers, could we be sure of obtaining huge profits. If just one of these competitive forces got out of control the company's profitability could be seriously affected, as its profits could leak out like air from a burst tyre: one tiny hole could cause the loss of all the air inside it.

Take the case of an industry that lacks one of these five forces. No matter which of these forces is removed, the industry could suffer the "flat tyre effect". Imagine that only rivalry is missing; the favorable situation of the rest of the forces would be pretty cold comfort, as there would be little profit to share out after the fratricidal struggle between the industry's companies. If the threat of new entries were the odd one out, because of the absence of entry barriers, the pull effect of the great profitability of the industry for new companies would be parallel to that of the honey-pot on the flies in the famous fable. If the five forces were lacking the existence of substitutes, the substitute industry would have the same effect on the profits of the industry as what is known as the communicating vessels effect, balancing the demand between the two industries through the price and thus putting a logical ceiling on the pretensions of the industry. Finally, it is not difficult to imagine what suppliers and customers do when they have great bargaining power over an industry with high profits (in which the other forces are controlled).

However, an industry does not usually have all five competitive forces in its favor, nor is it usual for just one to be missing. In most cases some of the forces will show some sign of weakness. The profitability of the industry will depend on the extent of this weakness. The final combination of the five competitive forces enables us to reach a conclusion about the nature of the industry's profitability.

But ultimately only three of the competitive forces indicate the profitability of the industry. In reality, profitability depends solely on rivalry, the threat of new entries and substitutes. The other two competitive forces, the bargaining power of suppliers and customers, show who gets to keep those profits – whether it stays in the industry or is transferred to its suppliers and/or customers.

How can we know the situation of each of the industry's competitive forces? How can we acquaint ourselves with the rivalry, the bargaining power, the substitutes, or the threat of new competitors that are at work in an industry? Through several factors. Each competitive force has a series of factors that will tell us its situation.

Some of these factors serve more than one of the forces, although their effect on each one may be different. For example, there might be a factor that serves to iron out rivalry, thus enhancing the profitability of the industry, but its effect on the threat of new entries might be to increase it, and this will undermine the profitability of the industry. Two opposite effects produced by the same factor on two forces. Therefore, when analyzing a competitive force and the situation of the factors affecting it, it is important to perform this analysis in total isolation, independently from the rest of the forces. This can sometimes be difficult, given the logical connection that exists between the forces and the factors that affect them.

5.3.1 Rivalry

The factors accounting for the rivalry to be found in an industry are as follows:

Number of competitors. Common sense tells us that the more competitors there are in an industry, the keener the rivalry. The industry will have to be shared out among more companies, and the portion (market share) will be smaller for each of them. As a result, the probability of attacks among these companies will be greater.

Balanced competitors. If the companies in an industry are of similar size and capacity the rivalry will be all the stronger, as they will all believe in the possibility of dominating the rest, and this will encourage aggressive actions. On the other hand, if there are some clear leaders, a few medium-sized enterprises, a number of smaller companies, and still others that are marginal, each firm knows its own position. The leaders set the pace; each company knows where it stands and is more cautious about launching an attack. Consequently, in such industries there will usually be less rivalry.

Growth. This is one of the factors that usually has most influence on rivalry. When an industry grows, the companies that comprise it only have to maintain their market share (their proportion of the industry's sales) to achieve an increase in their sales (equal to the growth of the industry). They achieve this increase without attacking any of their competitors. Therefore, the stronger the growth, the less rivalry there will be in an industry, as there will be less incentive to attack the other companies. This is so because it is simply unnecessary, since the increase in sales is achieved merely by maintaining the market share. Conversely, if we are considering a mature industry, with little or no growth, the only way a company can step up its sales is to increase its market share. To do this, it is obliged to attack its competitors, to capture customers from the rest of the companies in the industry. The most dramatic case occurs when the industry shrinks, because then companies are forced to attack their competitors just to maintain their sales. For example, 1,614,835 cars were registered in Spain in 2007, as opposed to 1,161,176 cars in 2008: 453,659 cars fewer, a drop of more than 40 percent. It is easy to picture the increase in rivalry in the dealership industry in Spain in 2008. The same can be said of the increased rivalry in the car manufacturing industry, as the slump also occurred Europe-wide and worldwide, although not so acutely as in Spain.

Fixed costs. To take an extreme example, if in a given industry there were no fixed costs – if all costs were variable – even if sales stood at zero there would be no loss, due to the absence of costs. Logically, all industries have some proportion of fixed costs (e.g. regular staff, debt redemption, rent, assets). The larger this proportion, the stronger the rivalry in the industry, as the companies that operate in it will be obliged to sell a higher proportion of their products or services in order to avoid having to bear the fixed costs of the unsold part. The hotel industry provides a clear example of this point, since in a hotel the proportion of fixed costs is quite high. If a hotel opens its doors, its costs are fairly similar regardless of whether it is full or empty. At times of slack demand rivalry becomes very keen, as hotels need quite a high occupancy to offset their fixed costs. This is why they have only two options in the low season: either close their doors, or lower their prices in order to try to achieve maximum occupancy.

Differentiation. In Chapter 3 we described differentiation as the strategy adopted by a company when it possesses a characteristic that is better than that of the competition and when this is perceived and appreciated by the customer – in a word, when the customer is provided with value. The more value provided by an industry through differentiation of one sort or another (such as quality, design, technology, innovation, service), the less this industry will have to resort to price to compete. On the other hand, in industries with very little differentiation, when all the companies offer the same thing, what competitive weapon remains to them? Unfortunately only price. Hence the greater the differentiation in an industry the less rivalry there will be.

Switching costs. These are the costs incurred by the customer of the industry simply as a result of changing supplier company. They refer solely to the costs of the switch (if there are any), and have nothing to do with the quality or price of the product or service. For example, in the cell phone industry a few years ago when customers changed operator they were forced to change number. This caused a switching cost for customers, inasmuch as when they changed operator they had to tell their professional contacts, family and friends their new number, with the associated waste of time and risk of losing contacts (and sales in the professional case). In short, this was a switching cost that dissuaded many customers from changing operators. Today this cost has disappeared, but contracting the service with a company still usually involves accepting a free or subsidized cell phone and signing a contract stipulating a minimum period which, if not fulfilled, obliges the customer to pay the full price of the phone. This also entails a switching cost for customers, since if they decide to change company they will have to bear the cost of the phone, which will not happen if they stay with their present operator.

Because they have to bear these switching costs, customers are less likely to change supplier, and so rivalry in the industry diminishes. Once a person has their bank, repair workshop or restaurants they trust, finding new ones means a cost in time, and also a risk. These too are switching costs that diminish rivalry because they stand in the way of changing company. The various types of loyalty programs (as used by airlines, hypermarkets, hotels, for example) pursue this effect of hindering change by creating a cost to make it (i.e. not reaping these benefits). To sum up, the higher the switching costs (or the greater the possibility of creating them), the less rivalry there will be in an industry.

Capacity. There is a logical relationship between demand and the instaled capacity of an industry. When there is overcapacity, rivalry shoots up, and the opposite happens when demand exceeds supply. This relationship between supply and demand is connected to some extent to the growth of the industry, but only in part. The growth of the industry refers only to demand (sales) and a time gap. The growth of the industry does not refer to supply (the industry's installed capacity).

Various competitors. If the companies in an industry do not have a proper understanding of each others' strategic behavior it may be misinterpreted, with the resulting risk of an increase in rivalry. For example, a company might sell a product at a low price to sell off its existing stock because it is making a new improved version, but the competition might interpret this low price as the start of a price war.

Strategic interests. If a company is in an industry for reasons other than the logical and normal one of making a profit, it may distort the rivalry in that industry. For example, a cosmetics firm may be in the pharmaceutical industry simply to gain prestige, rather than to make a profit. This firm will be prepared to lose money in the pharmaceutical industry to achieve this desired reputation for the cosmetics industry. Likewise, a corporation, diversified into several businesses, might be very interested in one of them because a strong position in that business will favor its situation in another business. This company will be willing to make a loss in this business for strategic reasons, as it will recover this loss in another industry. These actions increase the rivalry of the industry in which they are made. This phenomenon should not be confused with the logical losses made at the beginning, when a company enters an industry or is launching new products or services. In such cases the company is seeking to make a profit in the mid or long term, but it accepts that it order to achieve this it will have to make a short-term loss.

Exit barriers. Imagine an industry in which companies with losses and a disastrous competitive situation are unable to withdraw from it. These companies remain in the industry, where this inability to exit causes tension to rise steadily like the inside of a pressure cooker. As a result, rivalry increases. The higher the exit barriers surrounding an industry, the greater the rivalry within it.

An industry can have various types of exit barriers. First there are specialized assets, assets that have little liquidation value or high transfer or conversion costs. If a car manufacturer in a difficult competitive situation starts to weigh up the possibilities of leaving the industry, it will realize that part of its facilities is good only for making cars. With the industry in a situation of excess supply, such facilities are worth very little. If the company gets a low price for them, it will think twice before leaving the industry, as it will have to face major losses in this area. Furthermore, these facilities are the workplace of thousands of people whose redundancy pay will have a cost that may amount to many millions. This would constitute a second barrier, high fixed exit costs.

This car manufacturer might have other businesses that share a series of activities (e.g. administration, finance, management control, information systems) in order to obtain synergies and cut costs, as we saw in Chapter 1. These synergies and cost reductions would also disappear if it pulled out of the business, as the proportional part that it bore would be transferred to the remaining businesses. This is the third barrier, strategic interrelationships. Let us also suppose that the company is a third-generation family firm where it is up to the managing director, the founder's grandson, to decide about the closure. He might think he will go down in history as "the family failure who closed the business" and therefore might be reluctant to go ahead with it. This is an emotional barrier. Lastly, imagine the reaction of the government of the country of our fictitious company that is about to close, leaving thousands of workers unemployed, and imagine how the unions would take it. This is the fifth and last exit barrier, governmental and social restrictions.

5.3.2 Relationship between Factors: Weighting the Factors and Final Evaluation of the Force

When analyzing rivalry, and indeed all the other competitive forces, one of the most difficult aspects is how to think about each factor in isolation and independently. This is because some of them are related to each other. For example, if the industry shrinks, after a certain period of time overcapacity will usually result. This interrelationship occurs not only between the factors influencing a force; it also happens between the five competitive forces. If we think that some factors are reducing rivalry, it is also true that at the same time they are increasing the threat of entry by rendering the industry more attractive.

In conclusion, when we analyze a force we must try to do so in isolation, aseptically, without thinking about interrelationships or its effects on the rest of the forces. Equally, when we analyze a particular factor we should not think about how it affects the other factors that influence this force. We will take all its factors into account when we analyze and reach conclusions about the force. And similarly, we will take all its forces into account when we analyze and reach conclusions about an industry.

Once we have analyzed the factors accounting for rivalry in the industry, we must think about what key factors determine this force – which factors are true indicators of rivalry. As occurs with each of the five forces, not all factors are equally important. There may be factors that are unimportant in one industry (but crucial in another). These unimportant factors can be removed from the analysis. For example, in the industry concerned we might find that there are no switching costs, and that they are unlikely to arise in the future.

At the other extreme, although it is very improbable, it is possible that one single factor might be the key to determining the force, in this case rivalry. For example, in a monopoly rivalry stands at zero, and one single factor – the number of competitors – accounts for this lack of rivalry (because the answer to the question is zero). In this case one single factor is enough, and the rest are irrelevant.

Therefore, once all the factors that affect a force have been analyzed, they must be weighted. First, those that are irrelevant to the industry concerned must be removed (if there are any). Then we must judge which factor or factors have more influence on the force and which have less. For example, in many industries growth is a very important factor because when it changes, rivalry is different too. We need only think about the change in rivalry that might occur in an industry that grows 5, 10 or 15 percent one year and shrinks 30 percent or more the next year, as we have unfortunately witnessed in the recent crisis.

These factors that exert strong pressure on a force are not the only ones by any means. If necessary, several categories can be made according to the importance of the factors, always taking into account this weighting when making our conclusions about the situation of that force, evaluating the more significant factors more highly.

5.3.3 Threat of New Entries

In the threat of new entries there are two aspects to think about. The more important of the two is that of industry entry barriers, as ultimately it will be they that help or hinder entry into the industry, thus measuring the extent of the threat of new entries. However, we should also mention that companies that are considering the possibility of entering may think, before reaching a decision, about the reaction to their entry that can be expected from companies already in the industry.

The reaction to entry from the companies in the industry can be predicted on the basis of four factors. The history of past entries will provide objective data to assess. The resources available to the industry's companies will tell us how far their reaction could go. The present level of competition in the industry will give clues to go by. And lastly, the growth of the industry will reveal whether the "cake" is getting so big that the companies involved are unable to digest it, or on the contrary, whether the companies are hungry and unwilling to admit more guests to share the cake.

However, as we said earlier, **industry entry barriers** are what really protect the industry from new entries or expose it to them. Below we list the possible barriers to entry into an industry.

Economies of scale. When we introduced economies of scale in Chapter 3, we explained that the larger the company, the lower the unit cost. This effect can take place in all the activities of a company (R&D, operations, logistics, marketing). Logic tells us that when a company enters an industry it will not be very large, as it will have to attract custom gradually. And being smaller, it will have to bear higher unit costs than the companies already established in the industry in each of the activities that display economies of scale, which therefore constitute entry barriers. It is true that one company can buy another in the industry as a way of gaining entry to it, but in this case what it is doing is paying to acquire these economies of scale and to overcome the various other industry entry barriers.

Experience. Also in Chapter 3 we described the experience curve. In this case the decrease in unit cost was due to a gradual accumulation rather than greater size. The company has lower costs because of having been in the industry for many years, having experience, having learnt things over those years, and being more efficient. The new player will certainly not have experience in the industry, so it will have to bear the cost difference, and this constitutes a barrier. Two aspects must be taken into account with this factor. First, if the experience does not belong to the company itself but rather to people, this is not a major barrier, as the company that enters the industry can get round it simply by hiring people with this experience.

The other point to be borne in mind is that, as with the other entry barriers, if we are just talking about entry into a geographical market (for example the European Union) by a company that already belongs to the industry but in another region (say the USA), in many areas of the company it will take advantage of the experience accumulated in the first region. Perhaps not in all activities; in areas such as distribution, marketing or service it might be somewhat lacking in experience because of the specific characteristics of the new region, but its situation will in no way be comparable to that of a company that is new to the industry. As we said earlier, this reflection is applicable to the rest of the entry barriers.

Differentiation. This is a factor that we have already analyzed in connection with rivalry. We mentioned at the beginning of this chapter that there are factors that arise in more than one force. In these cases we should not qualify the factor again, but only its effect on the new force. Thus, if we concentrate on the role played by differentiation as an entry barrier we can conclude that the greater the differentiation the higher the barrier. By definition, companies that do not belong to the industry will not have this differentiation, and are obliged to achieve it. This is not easy, since acquiring any of the forms of differentiation (e.g. quality, design, technology, innovation, service, brand) is an extremely difficult feat.

If the new company is forced to differentiate itself, this will entail, as we have seen, heavier spending and possibly a greater need for know-how in some areas of the company: R&D, production, marketing and so on, depending on how it intends to differentiate itself (technology, quality, or brand image). For this reason, the risk it will have to take will be much greater, owing both to the greater resources and capacities that it has to invest in the attempt and also to the possibility that it may not achieve its objective of overcoming customers' loyalty to the companies that already belong to the industry. On the other hand, it is much easier to enter an industry without differentiation, with commodity products or services that are totally homogeneous and standardised (i.e. with no brand, technology, design, quality, service).

Capital requirement. The difficulty of entering an industry clearly increases the greater the need for financial resources. Opening a clothes shop, a fast food restaurant, a lighting fixtures shop or something along these lines is relatively cheap, and many people can afford to do so on an individual basis. At the other extreme, the manufacture of commercial aircraft is of an economic scope that renders it prohibitive even to large groups (quite apart from other aspects such as the necessary technology, which would belong in the above factor of differentiation).

Switching costs. This is another factor that appeared earlier when we were analyzing rivalry. This force is a clear barrier to entry since, as we have already explained, these costs are incurred by customers when they switch company, and therefore hinder this change. A company that enters the industry, being new to it, does not have customers, and so must always bear switching costs if they exist. The higher the switching costs, the higher the entry barriers.

Access to distribution channels. Companies reach their customers through a distribution channel – in the food industry through hypermarkets and supermarkets, in the car industry through dealerships, and so on. If a company that wants to enter the industry has major difficulties gaining access to its distribution channels, its entry will be virtually blocked as it will be unable to contact its end customer. Let us imagine a frozen food company that gives freezers to retailers in the industry free of charge on condition that they do not stock products in direct competition with theirs. Each freezer given away means a shop where competition has been blocked.

Patents. All the entry barriers discussed so far are barriers that can become important. However, patents have a special characteristic: they are barriers that are insurmountable, they cannot be overcome. If a patent actually works, the industry (or that part of it that is covered by the patent) becomes watertight; it is completely out of bounds to new players until it expires. However, when the patent does expire the barrier disappears completely. It is a game of all or nothing. For example, Xerox did not invent the photocopier, but it was the company that patented it (the first one to believe in the invention and buy it from the owner). While the patent was in force, Xerox enjoyed a privileged position. When the patent expired, dozens of companies entered the industry.

This is another example of what we explained earlier about the weighting of factors, when one or more factors may be enough to determine a competitive force. In the case of the photocopier industry described here, when Xerox's patent was in force, this single factor was enough to determine that the threat of entry by new companies was zero. In Chapter 3 we discussed the case of the success of Priceline.com, which was only possible thanks to the fact that the company patented the idea on which it was based, making access to the business impossible for other companies.

Favorable access to raw materials. Here we must understand raw materials in a broad sense, as, for example, natural resources, minerals, land, energy, water, components, manpower and financial resources. Logically, if one of these is very limited and is cornered by the companies already in the industry, it will constitute an important barrier against entry to that industry.

Locations. If entry to the industry depends on finding a certain location and it is difficult to come by, this becomes a barrier. When fashion firms enter a country they usually go for the main cities. There, they need to open their first shop in particular streets in the best areas, since flagship stores have to be on sites of exceptional prestige. If a suitable location is not available, they put off their entry until such time as it is.

Subsidies. Although they are becoming less and less plentiful due to competition rules, regulations and so on, subsidies awarded by various levels of government may form a barrier. However, they may also be an incentive for entry, depending whether they are offered to companies in the industry or firms from outside it who wish to gain access to it. In the latter case, obviously the situation of the industry is such that an incentive is required to make entry worthwhile, so its appeal cannot be very great.

Regulations. Again, they are increasingly uncommon, for the same reasons as above. Government relations and policies may be a barrier to an industry, a political barrier in this case. A market can be closed "politically", to a greater or lesser extent. This can happen through a range of measures: by banning imports totally, by setting tariffs, by establishing import quotas (limits), or by imposing specific tests or technical standards, and so on. The European Union brought the removal of all sorts of barriers among member states, but we still find them among the trade zones and/or countries of the world.

5.3.4 Bargaining Power of Suppliers and Customers

We will analyze these factors together, as they are virtually the same but seen from opposite perspectives (bargaining power of suppliers and bargaining power of customers).

Business concentration. The more concentrated an industry is (i.e. the fewer companies that comprise it), the more bargaining power it will have, as it will have more options to choose from. An industry made up of three companies with 100 suppliers is very different from one made up of 100 companies with just three suppliers. The extreme case is when the industry has only one supplier (or one customer). The power held by that supplier (or customer) under such circumstances is easy to imagine.

Substitutes. If an industry has substitutes it will have less power, as it is an industry that has alternatives; there are other industries that meet the same needs as it meets. The soft drinks industry has suppliers that can substitute each other, such as the plastic, glass, can or carton industries. Hence it wields a certain amount of power from this perspective, since in the event of one of these supplying industries having excessive demands at a particular time it will have another three to fall back on.

Proportion of sales/purchases. If an industry invoices a high percentage of its sales to one other industry, its dependence on that industry will cause its bargaining power to weaken. The opposite will happen if this industry accounts for only a small proportion of its sales. For this reason, car hire firms have high bargaining power because they buy large consignments of cars from makers, which translates as better prices for them than for a private customer.

Profitability. If an industry is going through a difficult patch, its interest in bargaining will be paramount, as it will be vital for it to try to pass on some of its losses to its suppliers or customers. Although in principle this factor is about an industry's interest in bargaining, in fact it sometimes explains the high bargaining power achieved. Considering the previous factor, the car's end customer has very little power (constituting a tiny proportion of a car maker's sales). This is so despite the fact that this consumer is very interested in this factor, as the car is the second largest purchase for a family after the home.

What do these customers do at times of crisis such as the period 2007–2011? Owing to their low profitability (purchasing power logically falls during a recession) and the poor prospects for the future, their interest in bargaining is topmost, as their resources are limited – so limited that if we consider them collectively they wield a deadly weapon: putting off their purchase, or in other words, repairing their old car. If we add up hundreds of thousands of decisions to put off buying a new car the result is a very serious situation for makers and dealers alike, as this sum of decisions not to buy spelt a 40 percent reduction in sales in Spain (even more in some regions) in 2008. The bargaining power of the end consumer at that time was enormous.

Differentiation. An industry that has differentiation has bargaining power. Differentiation involves value, value that is appreciated. In any industry, a supplier that contributes value will have bargaining power, as differentiation will help to improve the industry's product or service. Clear examples of this are quality restaurants that need suppliers of the finest produce and wines, or makers of premium cars and builders of luxury homes who need the most up-to-the-minute technological innovations. Any company needing a supplier that provides it with value, differentiation, will recognize that value, thus increasing the supplier's bargaining power. Owing to their extremely high differentiation, luxury companies in any industry have a great deal of power over their consumers, which enables them to set high prices. And the opposite happens when a company has undifferentiated products or services.

Switching costs. If a supplier has associated switching costs its bargaining power increases, because if its customers want to change supplier they will have to bear these costs. When we discussed these costs in connection with the first force in which they appeared, we gave the example of the cell phone industry; the fact that this industry involves switching costs gives it power over its customers. Switching costs makes it difficult to change operator because the customer has to bear these costs.

Threat of vertical integration. Just the threat of this integration, the fact of it even being feasible, is enough to increase bargaining power. If it is believable that the companies in a particular industry might become its suppliers or its customers, that industry acquires a supplementary bargaining power, as the existing suppliers or customers know that if there is no agreement the industry may decide to go ahead with the integration.

Information. It has always been said that information is power – all the more so if it is information about the "opponent" in a negotiation. The more we know about the costs, qualities, specificities, profitability and general situation of the supplier or the customer, the more bargaining power we will have.

5.3.5 Substitutes

As we have already mentioned, an industry is a substitute for another when it satisfies the same needs. We have discussed the case of the plastic, glass, can and carton industry, which all meet bottling needs.

In the case of substitutes, rather than the series of factors to consider, sometimes the essential point is whether an industry really has substitutes or not. We need to know whether another industry that can satisfy the same needs really exists. On occasion it is not so easy to find the substitute industry. A small business that makes Christmas and birthday cards – not only a very small company but also one with basic technology (a printing press) – might discover that its substitute is a huge, very high-technology industry. The telecommunications industry, particularly telephone companies, launches advertising campaigns encouraging the population to call their family and friends at Christmas time and even to wish them happy birthday.

Each person who decides to call their family and friends to wish them a merry Christmas or a happy birthday means one sale less for this card manufacturer. It turns out that this small enterprise with meager facilities and machinery, very little staff and basic technology, is making a substitute product with respect to large multinationals capable of multi-million dollar investments and possessing cutting-edge technology. So, as we observed earlier, sometimes the key in this force is to know whether the industry really has substitutes, and if so what they are.

Once the substitute industries have been detected, there are several factors to think about in order to evaluate the real threat they pose: price/quality ratio between these different industries; the profitability of each of them (this will account for the resources available to them to promote their products or services); whether the customer incurs costs on switching among the products or services of these industries (this will tell us whether they have a degree of forced loyalty); and lastly the user's propensity to substitute.

The substitutes we have discussed so far are known as functional substitutes. As we have explained, industries that satisfy the same needs perform the same function. However, there is another kind of substitute, known as non-functional substitutes. As their name suggests, they do not satisfy the same need, they do not perform the same function, but they may be chosen by customers as substitutes under certain circumstances.

To illustrate how non-functional substitutes work, let us take the example of John and his wife Mary, who after many years of hard work together have managed to buy their own home, provide their children with a university education and, on top of all that, save €70,000. John and Mary ponder about what to do with this money. Their first thought is for their eldest son, who finished university five years ago. John knows that an MBA would be extremely useful to him, as the combination of this with his engineering degree would give him great potential. But John also remembers that Mary is constantly saying that she has always wanted a little apartment on the coast, and that €70,000 would make a good down payment for that dream. John is also aware that his and Mary's cars (they both need one for their work) are both very old and could do with being changed; these new cars plus some repairs that would give the house a new lease of life are also

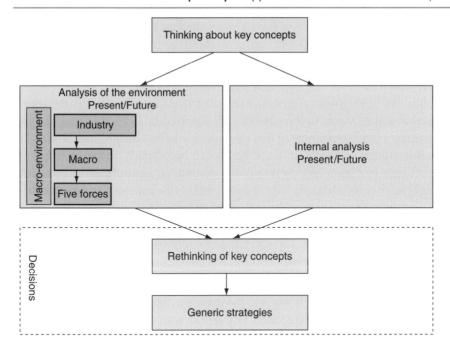

Figure 5.4 Addition of macro industry analysis to the GIB model

very valid options to invest the money they have saved. And lastly, our couple are aware that in a few years they will be retiring, and that a rational option would be to invest that money in pension plans for the two of them to prepare better for their future.

Mary and John only have €70,000, but they are thinking about investing this sum in such diverse things as an MBA, an apartment, cars and house repairs, and pension plans. In the end they will choose only one of these. These goods are non-functional substitutes, they satisfy very diverse needs, but Mary and John are deciding which of them to invest in; for them, they are all substitutes. Therefore, we also have to think about whether an industry might or might not have non-functional substitutes.

Figure 5.4 shows the addition of macro industry analysis to the GIB model.

5.4 Industry Life Cycle

In this chapter about the industry at the macro level, it is important to remember that industries, like products and services, also have a life cycle.

We will take the example of the industry of manufacturers of VHS videos, the format that won the initial battle fought in the industry against Betamax.

Introduction. When it was invented, video was unknown to the general public, so in the first stage it had to make itself known. This is the introduction stage, which in the case of video started in 1973. At this time few customers (end consumers in this case) decide to buy the product or service, as it is unknown. Furthermore, it has yet to be properly tried and tested as it has only just been launched onto the market, so any number of problems might arise. It is a trial period for both parties (the industry and its market). At this time there are usually few competitors due to its embryonic state; few companies have the capacity to provide the product or service, and furthermore few companies are interested in doing so, as its success has yet to be proven.

Growth. After a certain period of time the industry's product, in our case the video, becomes widely known, having been quite successful in the initial introduction stage. The customer is familiar with the advantages it brings, the needs it satisfies: in our case, being able to see the TV program of our choice without having to be at home when it is broadcast, or seeing a film at home since it can be rented and returned (which gave rise to another industry, the video rental industry). In this stage the product or service is gradually improved, as it is a stage of great growth in sales given the abovementioned existence of an incipient market. This results in the entry of competitors that will be the more plentiful the lower the entry barriers (as we have seen). This entry of competitors, if it is greater than the growth undergone by the industry, may cause rivalry to increase.

Maturity. After a period of growth, a day comes when almost all the customers in the market have the product or service. In our example, there came a time when there was a video in every home. Logically, the growth that the industry had enjoyed began to level off and eventually became almost flat. The disappearance of growth or, even worse, the beginning of the appearance of a fall in the industry's sales will depend on the replacement rate of the product or service. In the case of video, manufacturers tried to launch new models with better features in an attempt to encouraging replacement and thus soften the blow of this stage. Obviously the fall in growth increases rivalry in the industry, the struggle between companies in the industry being much fiercer just to maintain their market share. Companies are forced to put greater emphasis on costs in order to survive.

Decline. In our example, DVD (Digital Video Disc) suddenly appeared in 1997, bettering the features of video and having a disastrous effect on the video's sales figures. Sales started to fall to unsuspected levels. As a consequence of this, rivalry was extreme, to the extent that the companies in the industry started to beat a quick withdrawal. The market continued to shrink so fast that there were not enough customers to go round all the companies operating in it. At that time, the magnitude of the decline in the video industry mirrored that of the growth of the DVD industry. Manufacturers in the video industry tried to switch over to the new industry, seeing the grim prospects that awaited them.

Death. Once the alternative (DVD) is consolidated, it is only a question of time – and little time, at that – before the industry disappears altogether. Only a handful of customers remain for old time's sake, usually too few to allow any companies to earn a living, although a residual continuation may be possible in some cases, especially if the company also operates in the new industry, or this residual market is worldwide, or both. Figure 5.5 describes the key issues of the industry life cycle phases.

The life cycle curve can describe many shapes, and the length of each stage is completely different in each industry. For example, there might be another

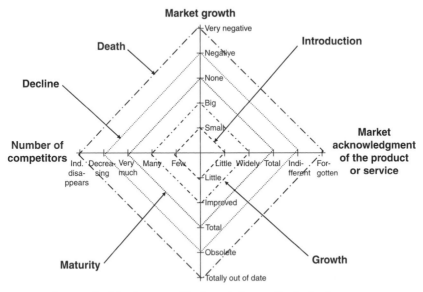

Figure 5.5 Key issues of the industry life cycle phases

growth stage after maturity, caused by major improvements in the product or service, or because the product or service is favored by some circumstance in the macro-environment. Equally, the maturity stage could last for many years. Another possibility might be a decline so slight that it is almost imperceptible. Or the life cycle curve might undergo ups and downs, forming a W due to the industry's reaction whenever there is a decline, introducing new developments that are appreciated by the market.

To sum up, each industry is different insofar as it has a different life cycle. The life spans of different industries are absolutely heterogeneous, as are each of their stages. There may even be some industries that think they are never going to disappear at all.

5.5 Questions for Reflection

I.   What is your industry? Define the industry in which you compete.[3]

II.   Would it be appropriate to change the definition of your industry (by narrowing it down, broadening it, or just changing it)?[4]

III.   What industry are you interested in analyzing (bearing in mind your industry definition)?

IV.   What is the current situation of the five competitive forces in the industry you have defined?

    a. Rivalry

       Factors accounting for this situation

    b. Threat of entry

       Factors accounting for this situation

    c. Bargaining power of suppliers

       Factors accounting for this situation

    d. Bargaining power of customers

       Factors accounting for this situation

    e. Substitutes

       Factors accounting for this situation

V. Consequently, what is the appeal/profitability of the industry at present? What main forces (and factors) account for this situation?

VI. How do you think the five competitive forces will stand in the future? (Set the time scale it would be logical to think about, considering the characteristics of your industry.)

    a. Rivalry

       Factors accounting for this situation

    b. Threat of entry

       Factors accounting for this situation

    c. Bargaining power of suppliers

       Factors accounting for this situation

    d. Bargaining power of customers

       Factors accounting for this situation

    e. Substitutes

       Factors accounting for this situation

VII. Consequently, what will the appeal/profitability of the industry be in the future? What main forces (and factors) account for this future change?

VIII. How might these future changes in your industry affect your company and its strategy?

IX. What should your organization do to prepare for this?

X. What stage in its life cycle is your industry in at the moment? How long do you foresee it continuing in this stage?

XI. When this change in the life cycle of your industry happens, what strategic changes will it bring to your company and its strategy?

XII. What should your company do to be ready when this change happens?

CHAPTER 6

Industry Analysis (II): Micro

As we have already mentioned, Guinness has been able to remain in its industry for more than 250 years. We cannot account for this with a macro industry analysis as presented in the previous chapter. To gain an insight into the competitive situation of Guinness (or any other company) we need a finer, more specific industry analysis.

We must focus on the industry with a higher-precision lens than in the macro analysis, a lens that gives us the possibility of delving deep into the industry to observe its micro-level detail, that enables us to observe all the companies in the industry – a magnifying glass that allows us to analyze the competitive situation and the strategic behavior of the industry's companies and thus understand the causes behind the profits they obtain. In doing so we aim both to grasp the reasons that account for this yield in the present and at the same time to predict how it will develop in the future.

In short, we want to be able to answer the question why in any industry some companies are more profitable than others. Why is Guinness today a global company with a strong competitive advantage, whereas other Irish beers such as Murphy's and Beamish do not share its competitive position, even though they too are stouts[1] and have been around for almost as long as Guinness?[2]

6.1 Strategic Dimensions

In order to gain a real insight into how an industry's companies compete, we must dissect its strategy further; we must dig deeper into it. The analytical concepts and tools described so far (see Figure 5.4) allow us to account for several different ways of competing. The generic strategies provided us with three very different strategies; they revealed three main strategic avenues.

In fact, the generic strategies separate an industry's companies into three main groups: those that follow a differentiation strategy, those that adopt a cost strategy, and those whose strategy takes the form of specialization. We could even make a fourth group: those companies that are "stuck in the middle", that want to apply more than one strategy but end up in the middle ground and actually achieve none of them. But let us suppose that all the companies are clear about their chosen strategy; let us keep these three well-defined strategic groups (we will return to the case of strategically inconsistent companies presently).

However, these three groups of companies, which will appear in any industry if we think of the generic strategies, are too broad for us to fulfill our current objective: to know the reasons for the different profitability of the companies in an industry. We need to dissect the strategy more precisely, go deeper into it, if we are to advance towards this goal. This tallies with what we were saying in Chapter 3: that these strategies were, as their name indicated, too generic, and so we would need greater strategic precision to get to know the strategies of many companies. In other cases we could not say which of the three generic strategies they followed.

Consequently we must continue to delve deeper into strategy, to which end we will add a new concept. This arises when we ask ourselves, within each of the three groups of companies we have dealt with so far (those that follow the respective strategies of differentiation, costs and specialization): do the companies in this group really compete in the same way? Or to be more exact, do all the companies that differentiate themselves compete in the same way? Do all those that follow a cost strategy do so in the same way? Do all the companies that specialize follow the same strategic path? Obviously, the answer is no.

If a company uses more strategic tools and concepts, it will obtain correspondingly greater depth in its thinking process, possess greater perspective and increase the clarity of its analysis. This becomes evident when we move on from the generic strategies to strategic dimensions, and therefore to the analysis of strategic groups. It is a step that adds depth, detail and clarity to the perspective that we had with the generic strategies. We said in Chapter 3 that the generic strategies were like three major motorways leading to a series of trunk roads, each of which led to a larger number of main roads, and so on. We are now coming to the trunk roads and main roads, the strategic dimensions.

6.1.1 Differentiation Dimensions

Not all companies that follow the differentiation strategy are the same, compete in the same way, or have the same results. And we can say the same about companies that pursue the cost strategy and those that seek to specialize.

If not all companies that differentiate themselves do so in the same way, it must be because they compete in several diverse ways, because they use different strategies. In order to understand this divergence we have to think about their competitive strategy, about how they compete.

As we also explained in Chapter 3, in any industry there are a multitude of ways of obtaining the differentiation strategy. Some companies might offer better quality, others excellent service, still others exceptional design, and yet others great capacity to innovate. All these roads lead to differentiation, but they are all totally different. The step we have just taken is the shift from thinking about generic strategies (in this case, differentiation) to thinking about strategic dimensions. Quality, service, design and innovation are strategic dimensions, in this case derived from the generic strategy of differentiation.

Obviously, a company may have more than one strategic dimension. Taking the example of Apple, we could say it competes in innovation using design and technology, all of which is supported by a brand name. This combination of four interconnected dimensions accounts for its strategy.

6.1.2 Low-cost Dimensions

The same reflection we have just made about companies that follow the generic strategy of differentiation can be made about those that follow low-cost strategy. If not all companies that follow this strategy do so in the same way, it must be because they compete in several diverse ways, because they use different strategies. Therefore, in order to understand this divergence, again we have to think about their competitive strategy, about how they compete.

In an industry there may be companies that have low costs because they achieve economies of scale; these will be large companies. Others may achieve low costs because of the experience curve; these companies will have been in the industry for a long time. And yet others achieve these low costs by having their own patented technology. Again, all three of these paths lead to the cost leadership strategy, but in very different ways. Economies of scale, the experience curve and technology are three

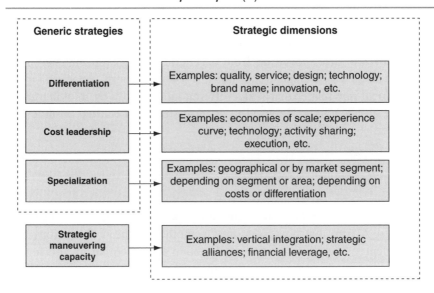

Figure 6.1 Examples of the shift from generic strategies to strategic dimensions

strategic dimensions, in this case derived from the generic strategy of cost leadership. Other sources of low costs, also discussed in previous chapters, include activity sharing, plant design, process improvement and a wide array of sources that are external to the company.

Logically, in this case too, a company can compete in more than one cost dimension. For example, being a large company (economies of scale) is not at odds with having accumulated years in the industry (experience curve) or possessing a better technology than the rest. A company could compete, for example, in all three of these cost dimensions. Figure 6.1 provides several examples of this shift from generic strategies to strategic dimensions.

6.1.3 Specialization Dimensions

In the third generic strategy the same reflection applies. Again, not all companies that specialize do so in the same way. As we have already explained, some specialize by market segment (needs), while others do so by geographical area. Within each of these two main types of specialization, each case differs greatly according to the segment (a sports paper or a business paper, for example) or the geographical area. And within each of these dimensions some companies will tend towards a cost leadership strategy, while others will opt for differentiation.

Again, we have moved on from a generic strategy (specialization) to how it is achieved: strategic dimensions. A low-cost sports paper is a far cry from a local newspaper that seeks differentiation. Only by thinking about strategic dimensions as opposed to generic strategies can we observe this difference.

6.1.4 Other Strategic Dimensions

So far we have described strategic dimensions that are derived from generic strategies. A firm that possesses one or another of these dimensions to a greater degree than its competitors will obtain a competitive advantage. If a company has higher quality or economies of scale or is better specialized in a market segment, that company has a competitive advantage (assuming that these dimensions are important in its industry, of course).

However, in Figure 6.1 we can see a fourth group of strategic dimensions that is not derived from the three generic strategies and therefore does not confer a competitive advantage directly. Nevertheless, these dimensions are important because they can help to achieve one of the others.

Hence they are dimensions that provide strategic maneuvering capacity (and are thus called). A company will not achieve a competitive advantage simply by deciding to make a strategic alliance. The implementation of this alliance will enable it to achieve an advantage: technology if the alliance is for research, or better distribution if it is in the area of logistics, for example. But it is not an advantage in itself. The same happens if we think about other dimensions that provide this strategic maneuvering capacity, such as vertical integration or a favorable financial leverage; they help to achieve a competitive advantage, but they themselves are not an advantage.

6.1.5 Understanding Strategy

Once we have taken this step from generic strategies to strategic dimensions, we can understand the strategy of all companies. We now possess a greater degree of accuracy, of strategic precision. We have their strategic ID card. This enables us to understand that there are companies that may be very clear about their strategy, but this strategy mixes strategic dimensions originating from more than one generic strategy, without these companies being "stuck in the middle".

For example, when we introduced the topic of differentiation dimensions we defined innovation as based on design and technology and supported by a brand name as a possible strategy for Apple; but note that Apple is also a large company and therefore enjoys economies of scale. Furthermore, it has been in its industry for many years and so enjoys an experience curve. In short, we could now say that Apple applies a strategy made up of the following dimensions: innovation, design, technology, brand name, economies of scale and an experience curve. This is a mixture of differentiation and cost dimensions, and is therefore difficult to place in any one of the three generic strategies. However, the firm is quite clear that above all it seeks differentiation, the cost dimensions serving to reinforce the search for that advantage, since the wider margin it provides is very useful in order to invest more in achieving its innovation, design, technology and brand.

A manifest increase in strategic clarity is achieved with this shift from generic strategies to strategic dimensions. We understand strategy much better; we can think about it more clearly since we are dealing with more strategic depth. We no longer have just three generic strategies but a whole range of strategic dimensions that can be combined with each other, yielding innumerable combinations that offer a large number of competitive possibilities.

This effect is achieved whenever we add a new concept, a new tool for analyzing the thinking process that we are following. It clarifies our position and broadens the strategic possibilities, especially if what is happening is related to the previous concepts that we have looked at. This is precisely what is intended to be the main contribution of the GIB model: to highlight the interrelationship of all the concepts and tools for analysis that are involved in the strategic formulation process.

6.2 Strategic Groups

Therefore, the strategic dimensions set forth in the section above will enable us to see the competition in an industry much more clearly, as we will have a sharp vision of the strategy of each company. If we focus on the strategy of each competitor, if we pinpoint its key strategic dimensions, those that confer competitive advantage, we will be able to group together competitors that follow the same strategy. The resulting cluster is known as a strategic group, as shown in Figure 6.2.

In an industry, the companies that compete most against each other are those in the same strategic group. By definition, they follow the same

Think Strategically

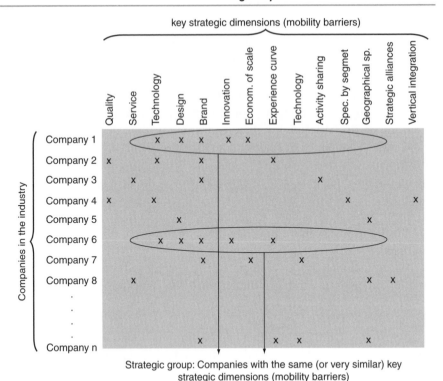

Figure 6.2 Examples of formation of strategic groups in an industry

strategy, they use and have the same key strategic dimensions, they target the same types of customers, and they seek to satisfy the same types of needs in those customers. In addition, there may be industries in which we find similar strategic groups with related strategies, also competitors to a large extent but never as much as companies in the same strategic group. In any event, strategic dimensions give rise to the formation of strategic groups, an essential tool for companies to know who their true competitors are.

At the other extreme, we can also imagine the case of two strategic groups whose companies, although they belong to the same industry, are not really competing against one another at all. Do sports newspapers and general-interest newspapers really compete against one another? Do Audi and Mercedes really compete against Tata? These groups of companies seek to achieve their competitive advantage in very different ways. They aim to attract very different customers, because they value very different aspects. They are in the same industry but we could say that they do not compete with each other.

The most successful and profitable strategic groups are those whose strategic dimensions are most highly valued by the market. These are the companies that will attract most customers, or customers that are willing to pay more, or both. And it is precisely their strategic dimensions that protect them in the long term from imitation by other companies in the industry.

If we go back to "Apple type" companies possessing innovation, design, technology, brand name, economies of scale and experience as an example of a profitable group, it should be noted that these dimensions are not easy to obtain. If a company is not in this strategic group it is because it does not possess these dimensions, and achieving innovation, design, technology, brand name, economies of scale and experience is no mean feat.

We could say that each strategic group has its own barriers to entry into that group, and these barriers are its own strategic dimensions. However, as they protect against the entry of companies that are already in the industry, they are not called entry barriers. They are called mobility barriers,[3] because they are dimensions that prevent a company from moving from one group to another. The strategic dimensions that constitute a mobility barrier in an industry are the key dimensions of that industry. They are to be taken into account when forming strategic groups, as they are the dimensions that provide the key to the industry's competitive advantages, and explain which companies have excellent competitive positions and why.

If we form strategic groups using dimensions that are not mobility barriers we will be joining together companies according to a way of competing that is irrelevant, as it does not confer competitive advantage. In reality these companies do not compete in the same way, yet we will be shoehorning them into the same group. In this case the groups that are formed, instead of informing us and helping us to understand the nature of competition in the industry, will actually mislead us. To quote an Argentinean advertisement from a few years back, "It's better to have no information than to think you have it" – an awful truth that can have disastrous consequences for a company.[4]

It is essential for the strategic groups to be formed on the basis of key strategic dimensions, dimensions that constitute mobility barriers (as shown in Figure 6.2). This is the key step for the analysis of strategic groups; we cannot afford to get it wrong. If we are not sure about which dimensions are mobility barriers in an industry it is better to stop the analysis – and start to worry about our lack of knowledge.

In short, strategic dimensions and the strategic groups that are formed on the basis of them give us a transparent picture of the competition in an industry. They tell us clearly who is in competition with whom. They group together the companies that really have maximum competition with each other, and furthermore tell us the various forms that competition takes in an industry.

From the above we can deduce that if a company wants to satisfy several market segments – that is, dissimilar groups of customers – each with different needs, it will employ several strategies, several clusters of strategic dimensions. Therefore, it will be in different strategic groups, competing against different companies, or against the same companies also using different strategies.

By way of example, we can mention the Accor Group in the hotel industry, which is present in several strategic groups. As a result, the group implements a variety of strategies in order to be able to target several market segments, as shown in Figure 6.3: luxury with Sofitel; different strategies of medium–high quality hotels (Pullman for business and Novotel, aimed more at families); quality strategies through the brands Mercure, Suitehotel and Adagio, the latter for apartment hotels); others targeting economy segments, with more attention to costs (All Seasons and Ibis); and lastly, clearly cost-oriented strategies for low-budget segments (Etap and Formule 1, and Motel 6 in the USA and Canada).

Logically, a company may perform one strategy well, it may be successful in one strategic group, but less so in another strategy; it may be unable to be so competitive in the other strategic group. A few years ago British Airways, taking note of the market shares and the profits that were being attained by low-cost airlines, decided to enter this strategic group. To do

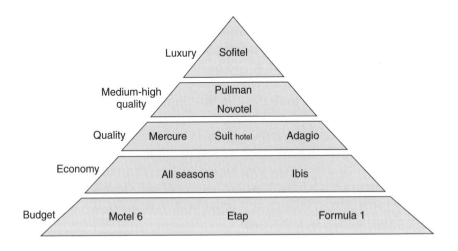

Figure 6.3 The Accor Group as an example of a company that operates in several strategic groups (using different strategies)

this it set up the company Go, only to sell it to easyJet a few years later (in 2001) in view of its disappointing results in the new strategic group.

6.3 Mobility Barriers and Profitability of Strategic Groups

As we mentioned earlier, each strategic group has its own barriers to entry into that group (mobility barriers), which are the same as the group's strategic dimensions. In fact, mobility barriers, being barriers (albeit internal ones), are the same factors as we were analyzing in the previous chapter with regard to entry barriers. Think of the dimensions we listed for Apple: innovation, design, technology, brand name, economies of scale and experience. The first four are differentiation dimensions, and like the last two (economies of scale and experience) they are entry barriers, as we saw in Chapter 5.

This is the first reason accounting for why some strategic groups are more profitable than others. These groups are protected by mobility barriers (barriers to entry into the group). This has similarities to the macro industry analysis we conducted in the previous chapter. There, the five competitive forces accounted for the profitability of the industry as a whole. This being the case, in view of everything we said in that chapter about industry analysis at the macro level, it is also true to say that these same five forces explain why each strategic group has different profits. This is so because the five forces affect each group differently.

We have already seen that the barriers to entry into each group are different. Is rivalry the same in each strategic group? Obviously not. For example, one group might be made up of a large number of balanced companies, with little differentiation and little growth, while another group might consist of a small number of highly differentiated companies undergoing vigorous growth. Two worlds, two completely different rivalries.

We will observe the same contrast with regard to the rest of the competitive forces. A strategic group made up of highly differentiated companies that provide their customers with added value (for example, a strategic group that can be classified as "luxury" in any industry) will usually have bargaining power over its customers, as these customers appreciate – they even demand – this value they are offered. The opposite extreme would be a group comprising undifferentiated companies whose customers are unappreciative of the little value they receive; such a group will usually have little bargaining power over its customers.

The bargaining power wielded by these typical groups over their suppliers will usually be the opposite of that we have described over their customers. Thus the strategic group formed by highly differentiated companies will have suppliers that will in turn offer them differentiation, as they will need high-value products or services to devise their own tremendously differentiated option. Furthermore, we will usually find few high-value suppliers. As a result, these companies will appreciate the value they are offered by their suppliers, who will hold strong bargaining power (unless the other factors in the negotiation offset this power). Again, the opposite will be the case with the undifferentiated group. Usually its suppliers will not offer them value and so their bargaining power will tend not to be very high.

Lastly, it is also possible that one strategic group might have substitutes, whereas another might not. In short, the five competitive forces affect each strategic group differently, making the profitability of each group different.

At this point we may be faced with another question: why don't companies in an unprofitable strategic group join a more profitable one? Or to say the same thing differently, why don't companies in less favored groups imitate the strategic dimensions of the better groups? The answer is as clear as it is simple: because they can't. All we need is to come full circle and remind ourselves that one of the five forces that act differently on the different groups is that of barriers to entry into them (mobility barriers) and that they impede this movement. In fact, that was the graphic reason for calling them mobility barriers.

With this insight into how companies such as Walmart in distribution, Coca-Cola in drinks and McDonald's in fast food compete, we can understand how they can continue to be leaders in their industries for so many years, more than a century in the case of the Atlanta-based firm, and more than half a century in the other two cases. Their own strategies, their own strategic dimensions, protect them. But it is also true that 100 years of domination do not guarantee even so much as one year more. Care must always be taken because, as we have already mentioned, all analyses are snapshots that are only valid for the instant they are taken. The competitive situation is absolutely dynamic; it changes with great rapidity. Hence, from this perspective, the strategy of a company in a strategic group with a very good competitive position should be to raise the mobility barriers of its group and/or create new equally or even more daunting barriers.

6.4 Strategy Maps

Strategic groups can be presented graphically for ease of understanding. This is what we call a strategy map. It is a two-dimensional matrix, each dimension representing the values of two strategic dimensions. The groups are already known (we have formed them by grouping together companies with the same or very similar mobility barrier dimensions), and the advantage of these maps is to display them visually.

The fact that a strategy map is limited to two dimensions explains the plural form of the title of this section. One single strategy map will hardly ever be enough to understand the situation of the groups in an industry. If it were, it would mean that just two strategic dimensions would be sufficient to know the keys to the industry's situation. And as we have already discussed, there will usually be many more than two mobility barrier strategic dimensions.

Figure 6.4 shows a simplified example of a strategy map of the sparkling wine industry (cava, champagne and other sparkling wines) in Spain in 2009, based on a case study[5] of the industry.[6] As we have already explained, in order to provide a complete overview of the industry this would not be sufficient in itself and would have to be completed with other strategy maps.

In this example we can see that the selected strategic dimensions are the quality of the products made by the companies in the industry and these products' brand image. Seven strategic groups appear. It is important to take into account what we said earlier to the effect that one company may belong to more than one strategic group. For example, a firm might invoice a large number of units in the strategic group "popular cavas", but it may also be present in the groups "traditional cava" and "intermediate cava", and it

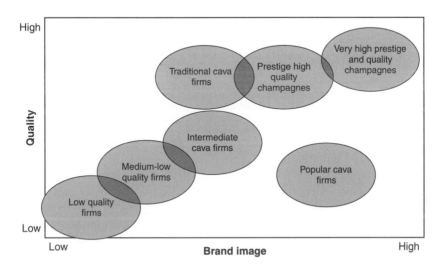

Figure 6.4 Example of strategic groups in the sparkling wine industry

Source: Franch, Gimbert, and Cano

might even be in the champagne groups. Logically, a company would have different brands in each group, since by definition the strategy of each group is different and brand name is one of the dimensions whereby differentiation is achieved in each strategic group. In this industry, presence in more than one strategic group means different brands for each one. This is usually the case; different brands are owned in each group, as this is how the range of products is presented to the customer. However, there are other industries in which a single brand name is used to implement several strategies. For example, in the case of computer manufacturers, it is the model that reveals the difference (this doesn't mean that there is not brand differentiation).

With the example in Figure 6.4 we can understand how strategy maps help to explain the situation of the various strategic groups and to think about future possibilities. For example, if we look at this strategy map we can see how there are cavas with a quality equivalent to that of champagne but which still enjoy less prestige. This could provide an idea for strategic development, a path to pursue.

We might also find that the strategy map highlights a space that is still unoccupied. This is not the case of the example in Figure 6.4, since the only area without companies is the top left-hand corner, an area that no company wants to occupy, because it would correspond to high-quality firms with a low brand image, obviously a suicidal strategy.

On the subject of the abovementioned limitation of two strategic dimensions per map and the resulting need to make more than one strategy map (because there are usually more than two mobility barrier dimensions), there are a couple of points to bear in mind. First, an industry does not usually have a very excessive number of dimensions that constitute major mobility barriers (key dimensions for success, as they provide long-term competitive advantage insofar as they cannot be imitated, thus explaining the diverse profitability of the industry). In the above example, quality and brand image undeniably fulfill these requirements; it is very difficult for a firm that is only in the group "low quality" to move to the group "traditional cava" or even the group "intermediate cava".

Secondly, sometimes there are dimensions that are correlated, that move at the same time. For example, returning to Figure 6.4, if we remove the strategic group "popular cavas" we are almost left with a diagonal line (which would become a perfect one if we also removed "traditional cavas"). If a strategy map depicts a diagonal line, the two dimensions that comprise it are correlated. In our example, this correlation would mean that, in this industry, the higher the quality of its companies (and hence its strategic groups), the better their brand image. In this case, quality and brand image would be correlated strategic dimensions.

In such cases the two correlated dimensions can be set along a single axis, as they move at the same time. This correlation can be positive, as in the example here, where an increase in one dimension is matched with an increase in the other, or it can be negative, one dimension decreasing as the other increases. This could occur, for example, with the dimensions cost and quality. If this happened, it would mean that those strategic groups with higher quality incur higher costs.

It should also be taken into account that the selected dimensions need not be continuous, in the sense of being measurable gradually (from 0 to 100, or from high to low). For example, if we study the soft drinks industry, we can select the dimension "channel", in which we will distinguish hypermarkets, supermarkets, neighborhood shops, bars, restaurants and so on.

A strategy map can be used as a starting point for thinking in various directions. Perhaps the most obvious one would be the competitive situation of each group: which is in the most favorable situation and why? Which mobility barriers will be longest lasting? What general expectations does each group have? Is there a marginal group, in a desperate situation?

We can also think about the situation and the reaction of the various groups in the face of different trends or scenarios. For example, how does a crisis such as that of 2007–2011 affect each group? Which are most affected? What strategic changes can they make to avoid its consequences? How can they be expected to react? In what direction will they try to move? Other trends worth thinking about might include globalization, the growing importance of emerging countries, global warming, and the increase in life expectancy, among others. Depending on the type of industry, some trends will be more important than others.

Consequently, we could try to predict possible competitive movements, changes in dimensions and groups; detect the creation of new groups; or find ourselves an "unfilled strategic gap" that might represent a good opportunity.

6.5 Closing the Circle of Industry Analysis

Figure 6.5 shows the situation of the GIB model following the addition of micro industry analysis. The figure shows that the macro industry analysis (five forces) is completed by adding its other (micro) part and in this way we close the circle of industry analysis. We observe that as a consequence of the micro analysis (strategic groups) we are faced with a decision about the strategic dimensions the company seeks to pursue. As we have argued, this

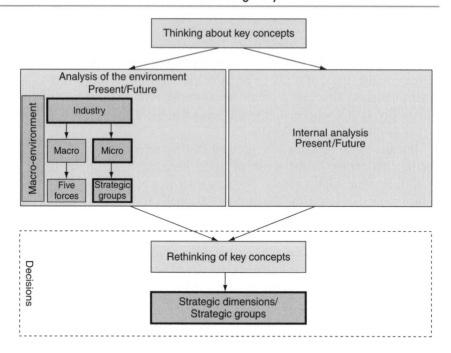

Figure 6.5 Addition of micro industry analysis (strategic groups) and the decisions derived from it to the GIB model

is a strategically much more complete decision than generic strategies, and it should be noted that the latter have therefore been removed in Figure 6.5 and replaced with strategic dimensions. It would be totally redundant to keep both concepts.

From this perspective of industry analysis, we could define strategic formulation as "choosing which strategic group the company wants to compete in" – group or groups because, as we have seen, a company can belong to more than one group, by implementing more than one strategy. For this reason, the strategic group also appears in the decisions section. In fact this is implicit in the decision about strategic dimensions, but at this stage in the process both are highlighted.

Furthermore, this perspective of industry analysis enables us to break down a company's results into as many as four levels. First, they will depend on the industry in which it competes: the more attractive or profitable the industry is, the higher the firm's profits will be. The second level depends on the strategic group in which the company competes: the better its competitive position (i.e. the more profitable and protected by barriers it is), the higher the firm's profits will be. Third, not all the companies in a strategic group are the same, they do not achieve the dimensions that unite them by the same methods; some companies are always better than others in any strategic group. Therefore the third level is the firm's competitive position within its strategic group. Lastly, we know that strategy is dynamic, it is written every day. It will depend on how the strategy of the company develops, how it evolves over time.

We have already discussed how all the tools for analysis in the GIB model are like snapshots, valid for the moment they are taken. Therefore we also know that, in addition to the current snapshot, we need to take another one of the future. Clearly this is also true for micro industry analysis, the analysis of strategic groups.

6.6 Questions for Reflection

I. What strategic dimensions does your company's strategy have?

   a. Differentiation dimensions

   b. Cost dimensions

   c. Specialization dimensions

   d. Strategic maneuvering capacity dimensions

   If your company has more than one strategy, define as many sets of strategic dimensions as strategies it has.

II. Consequently, what strategic groups does your company compete in?

   a. Strategic group

   b. Dimensions of the group

   c. Companies that belong to this group

   d. Situation of these companies within the group

   Again, if your company has more than one strategy in this area, you should define as many strategic groups as strategies it has.

III. What other strategic groups are there in the industry that may be of interest to you (because they are potential groups for your company in the future, because they are the most powerful groups in the industry, because there is a certain amount of intergroup competition, because some of your main competitors are in them)?

   a. Strategic group

   b. Dimensions of the group

   c. Companies that belong to this group

   d. Situation of these companies within the group

  IV. What situation and expectations do you think each strategic group has? What strategic groups do you think are in the best competitive position (e.g. because they have the strongest and longest-lasting mobility barriers, because they have higher sales and/or margins)? Are there any marginal groups?

   V. How will possible future changes detected in the macro environment affect each strategic group?[7] Pay special attention to those groups in which your company competes.

  VI. Make some strategy maps of the industry (with the main dimensions, those that are powerful mobility barriers).

  VII. Is there a "strategic gap" in the sector, a potentially interesting strategy that is not implemented by any of the companies?

VIII. What future movements do you think will occur among the strategic groups in your industry?

   a. Strategic group in which changes will occur

   b. Companies in the group that will be involved in these changes (unless it is the whole group)

   c. Possible future movements of these

   d. Possible change in the strategic dimensions of the group as a whole e. Changes in the importance of the groups (due to variations in their sales and/or margin potential, or in the importance of their mobility barriers)

Do this exercise as many times as there are groups of interest to your company that you think may undergo changes in the future.

CHAPTER 7

Market Analysis

From 1996 to 1999 General Motors produced and leased its first electric car, the legendary EV-1. It was a car destined to mark the beginning of a new technological era in Detroit. But then it suddenly disappeared from the market (possibly due to pressure from the oil industry) and General Motors decided to pursue the opposite strategy, making insatiable fuel hogs like the four-wheel drive Hummer. This was a fatal error because its customers wanted smaller, more efficient cars, not gas guzzling monsters – and it led General Motors to bankruptcy in June 2009. The market is strategically crucial. Any company that fails to produce what its market wants is sentenced to suffer a terrible and irremediable punishment: the market's indifference toward what that company is offering it. After a certain amount of time with the company persisting in its error, this punishment will ultimately result in the company going under, as General Motors discovered so traumatically, in common with another Detroit giant, Chrysler, which collapsed in April 2009.

So, when General Motors and Chrysler eventually rose up from the ashes, they started to ask themselves what their market was demanding. As a result, Chrysler made an alliance with Fiat to acquire the necessary technology and know-how to make small, efficient cars. And the new General Motors opted, among other things, for a new electric car, the Chevrolet Volt.

7.1 The Market

In the strategic jigsaw puzzle that we are building through the GIB model, the market is essential; without it, there is no possible strategy. The industry exists because the market exists. Companies are created, developed and maintained because they have customers to target. Companies supply because customers demand. Because of this, this analysis is intimately linked to the previous one; market analysis is tightly enmeshed with industry analysis.

When embarking on the latter, we asked ourselves whether all companies were the same, whether they practiced the same strategies. As the answer was obviously no, we separated the companies in any given industry in terms of their way of competing, their strategic dimensions, subsequently grouping together those that had the same dimensions, thus forming what we call strategic groups.

In market analysis the unit is not the company but the customer. But we ask ourselves the same question at the outset: are all the customers in a market the same? In this case they will not be the same because they act the same, as was the case of the companies in an industry. In this case they will be the same if they request, if they demand, if they value the same goods, because whereas the industry is the supply, the market is the demand. The answer to that question is just as negative as it was in the case of the industry. In a market the customers are not the same. The demands, needs, tastes, circumstances, purchasing power, age and so on of customers are so different that their combinations usually offer several different groups of customers.

These groups of customers who value or need the same goods are known as market segments. And what those customers appreciate or need are known as key success factors. Consequently, this chapter belongs to the area of marketing. In it we will set forth the essential points of this area to be taken into account when engaging in a strategic thinking process at the business level: which of the many pieces that go to make up the universe of marketing must be added to the strategic jigsaw puzzle that the GIB model is building at the business strategy level. The answer comes down to just two concepts. All areas of marketing are important for a company, but when undertaking a process of strategic thinking, when thinking, or rethinking, strategy at the business level, two marketing concepts are essential: segmentation and key success factors (KSFs). We will add these factors to the GIB model in the area corresponding to the market, as shown in Figure 7.1.

If the marketing department of a company segments a market incorrectly, when defining which groups of customers belong to it and/or what those customers value or need (KSFs), the whole strategic jigsaw puzzle comes apart. If we do not know who our customers are and/or what they want, how can we define the right strategy? Impossible. We will be as lost as if we were driving around the steppes of Kyrgyzstan without a GPS.

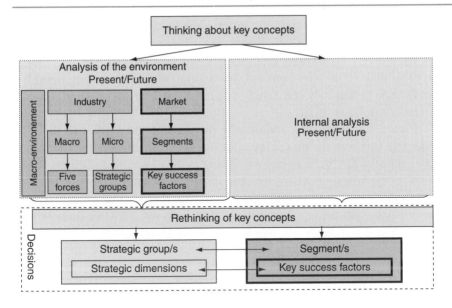

Figure 7.1 Addition of market analysis (segmentation and key success factors) and the decisions derived from it to the GIB model

The parallel between industry analysis and market analysis is obvious. The industry is made up of companies that offer, make goods, through their various strategies (strategic dimensions); it is the supply. The market is made up of customers who request, need, value goods; it is the demand. A group of companies that act similarly, that have the same strategy, that carry out the same strategic dimensions, is called a strategic group. A group of customers who demand, who request, the same goods is called a market segment. In short, if the component of the industry is the company, that of the market is the customer. If companies are grouped according to how they act (their strategic dimensions), customers are grouped according to who demands the same things, their key success factors.

However, between the industry and the market there is more than just similarity. As we mentioned at the beginning of this chapter, the two are intimately linked. In fact, if we have already seen that the company exists because it has customers and it makes goods because its customers demand them, we can go one step further and say that a company carries out a strategy in order to satisfy its customers' needs. Therefore, there is a connection between strategy, strategic dimensions and the customer's demand in the form of key success factors. Hence there is also a link between strategic groups and segments.

More specifically, a strategic group aims to satisfy the needs of, above all, a market segment. Furthermore, the strategic group exists, it carries out its strategic dimensions (and is therefore a group) because the companies that make it up have detected that a group of customers (segment) has needs (KSFs) that they can satisfy (with their strategy, with their strategic dimensions).

Figure 7.1 shows the addition of the area of the market to the GIB model. In this way the model includes market segmentation and the reason for it, namely, key success factors. Owing to the close relationship between them, as explained above, in the area of decision-making the segment that the company wishes to target is associated with the strategic group to which the company will belong, just as the KSF it seeks to satisfy are linked to the dimensions it will carry out. We will examine both these connections on a practical level in the following section.

7.2 Segments and Key Success Factors

Let us consider a very popular market: cars. Our tastes as consumers of this product (customers of the market) can vary widely. The design, engine power, space, toughness and so on of a car are valued very unequally by different people. Furthermore, we have widely differing lifestyles that influence our assessments. But at the same time we are conditioned by a host of factors, such as our family situation. It is not the same to have a family with four young children as it is to be single or divorced with no children. And, alas, it is not same to be 50 years old as it is to be 20. Or to need a car for frequent long trips as opposed to short journeys in town. Or to live in a village in the mountains as opposed to a city. And as we are so painfully aware, it is not the same to be on a minimum wage as it is to be a multi-millionaire.

All these diverse characteristics are examples of segmentation variables, in this case of the car market. By combining them, we form segments of this market. It is easy to imagine that a considerable number of different segments will result, each of them valuing very different aspects of the car.

If our customer is industrial, the segmentation variables will be rather different. Instead of age, family situation or lifestyle, we will have to consider variables such as size, type of industry, required technical sophistication or service, location, economic capacity, required distribution channel, frequency and procedure of purchase, and so on (depending on the industry, naturally).

As we have already mentioned, the responsibility for introducing this essential ingredient into strategic thinking at the business level lies with the marketing department. This is why the marketing department tends to be such a crucial area of the company. Furthermore, it is responsible not only for segmenting the market but also for subsequently communicating to it the strategy decided by the company; getting across to the customer that he is being offered what he needs.

Once segmentation is complete, company management has a great strategic responsibility. This segmentation provides it with a "menu of strategic possibilities". From this menu it must choose the dish or dishes it wants to try to taste and digest. Returning to the example of the car market, we can imagine the large number of segments facing a manufacturer – a manufacturer or indeed a dealer, because although the latter might appear to be limited by the makes for which it has a distribution agreement, it should perform this exercise thinking primarily about what sort of consumer it wants to attract.

So, in the analysis section of the GIB model (see Figure 7.1) we are faced with this "menu of strategic possibilities". This menu has two components, one being the consequence of the other. First, the segmentation of the market: which different groups of customers it is broken down into. And second, the key success factors of each of those segments, in other words, the reasons why each segment is different. The strategic thinking by company management about the market at the analysis stage should be: out of all these possibilities, all these segments, which should our company target? It must ask itself this question in the knowledge that each segment exists insofar as it values or needs a set of KSFs, factors that the company must necessarily satisfy better than its competitors if it decides to target that segment. This thinking is essential and far from easy, since sometimes segments are as numerous as they are diverse.

Thus, for example, by combining the segmentation variables of the car market we mentioned earlier, we can describe such dissimilar segment profiles as: "young single man with limited purchasing power who values engine power and sportiness", "family with young children who give priority to space", "company executive who needs a prestige high-performance company car", "sales representative who requires a cheap comfortable car capable of high mileage without breakdowns", and "middle-aged person on a minimum wage living in the country". As we all know, there are many more segments, but with these five alone we can already conclude that five different strategies are required, five absolutely different cars, concepts, messages and so on.

And the reason why these strategies are so dissimilar is that the KSFs of each segment are very different. For example, in the case of the "young single man" they might be price, design (sportiness), engine power and a minimally sporty brand image. In turn, for the "executive" they might be high performance in all the car's features, luxury and a brand image with an extremely high reputation. Quite the opposite is true for the "family with children", for whom the KSFs could be space, comfort, safety and fairly reasonable value for money.

This is the type of thinking that should be performed in the analysis stage, in order to be able to make the right decisions from this market perspective: what segment or segments the company is going to target, and therefore what KSF it will be able to satisfy better than its competitors. As explained earlier and reflected in Figure 7.1, these decisions are linked to those concerning the industry: what strategic dimensions we are going to carry out, and therefore what strategic group or groups we are going to compete in.

Thus, continuing with the example of the car market, if the Volkswagen Group wants to target segments that value (i.e. with KSFs of) very high quality, technology, innovation and design, it will do so with strategies that include this very high quality, technology, innovation and design as their strategic dimensions. The Volkswagen Group targets the segments described with several strategies through the company Audi. This involves several segments, as this part of the market that values very high quality, technology, innovation and design can in fact be broken down into several groups of consumers. Each of them is sporty, family-oriented, outdoorsy or whatever to differing degrees, and they have different ages, family situations and purchasing powers.

On the other hand, if the Volkswagen Group wants to target segments that are more price-conscious, it will have to carry out strategies that, without neglecting the dimensions already mentioned, pay more attention to the dimensions of costs. In this case it does so through the company Škoda. Similarly, it redesigned the strategies of SEAT when it decided to aim the brand at sportier segments. And it targets consumers with extremely high purchasing power who value maximum quality, technology, innovation and design in sports models with strategies that match these key factors through Lamborghini.

In short, if, in an extreme case, a company wants to target all the segments in a market, it will have to be in practically all the strategic groups – perhaps not all, because there might be some marginal groups that manage to hang on with practically no competitive advantage. No company would choose to be in one of these.

As the Volkswagen Group seeks to target virtually all market segments, it owns such widely contrasting car makers as Bentley, Bugatti, Lamborghini, Audi, Volkswagen, Seat and Škoda (as well as Volkswagen

Commercial Vehicles). As we have already discussed, one of the key success factors of a market is brand image. In the car market, the consumer does not only demand a series of characteristics in the vehicle; he also expects the brand of the car to communicate a whole world, a world that he appreciates. A Bentley without its symbol, without its striking and prestigious winged "B" and with the badge of a brand of utility vehicle instead, would be exactly the same product but would be worth much less.

This market view of strategy should make the company think about the investments it makes. To simplify, a company can make two kinds of investments. Some are obligatory, as they are necessary to be in an industry, to operate in it. These would include having a certain level of staffing, facilities and so on. However, other investments are made with the aim of achieving differentiation. A company must be sure that every cent it spends on differentiation is going to improve the satisfaction of a key success factor, and that this KSF has enough customers in its segment for this investment to yield a return. If this is not the case, the investment will not really be an investment at all; regrettably, it will just be a cost.

Nevertheless, it should also be borne in mind that sometimes customers are still unaware of the existence of a need, especially in the case of totally innovative products or services that they are obviously unfamiliar with. Products like the Walkman and the Minivan were not valued by consumers according to market research before they were launched. And as we all know, they were very successful.

7.3 Minimum Success Factors

In a market, in a segment, there are not only key success factors, there are also minimum success factors (MSFs). No one likes to stay in a hotel, no matter how cheap it is, in which safety and cleanliness are not guaranteed. Having a stranger come into your room while you are asleep, or jeopardizing your health due to the deplorable condition of the room, is not usually accepted. Safety and hygiene are minimum success factors in the hotel market. In fact, safety and hygiene are minimum success factors in all the markets in which they can be relevant, such as food, drinks, transport, construction, leisure and so on.

These are examples of minimum factors that are there and have always been there. But we might also find that a key success factor becomes a minimum one (and vice versa). Think of a market segment in which quality is key. As it is a KSF, the companies in the industry that target this segment will constantly invest to improve the quality they offer, because the strategic game from this market view we are taking consists of just that: detecting KSFs and satisfying them better than the competition does. In this way the quality offered to the segment or segments that value it will rise over time.

After a certain period of time, the quality offered might have developed to such a degree that the customer of that segment (or those segments) ceases to demand any further development. At that moment, that KSF (i.e. quality) will have reached the upper threshold desired by the market, thus becoming an MSF.

The reverse process, the shift from MSF to KSF, could also happen. Imagine that technology is a minimum requirement in a given market segment, as the companies that target it have approximately the same level of technology. However, a time comes when one of them develops a new technology that is appreciated by that segment. This technological innovation causes this dimension to become a KSF of the segment once again. As we know, all strategic variables are profoundly dynamic; they change. MSFs should not be seen as static. All companies should think of whether they are capable of turning an MSF into a KSF as one of their strategic possibilities.

Both KSFs and MSFs are appreciated by the market. If a variable is not appreciated by the market it will not come under either of these categories. The difference between them is that whereas the KSF distinguishes positively, rendering some companies better than others, the MSF distinguishes negatively, possibly causing some companies to disappear from the segment. Another difference is that in the case of the KSF the segment expects more, it has expectations of a possible improvement of the factor and is willing to pay for it; it appreciates this improvement. In contrast, in the case of the MSF the segment does not expect more; it is a minimum (as its name indicates) that is taken for granted in all the segment's products or services. Air Madrid disappeared from the airline industry for not fulfilling the industry's minimum requirements of punctuality and safety. The fulfillment of the MSFs of the market is an inexorable law.

In short, when we analyze some of the KSFs of a market segment, we tend to find that the companies that target it do so unequally. We will usually observe that some satisfy it better than others; this is precisely what competition is all about, as we have already discussed. However, if we focus on an MSF of a segment, we will see that all the companies that target that segment satisfy that MSF to an equal extent – precisely the minimum level demanded by the market, since the companies that do not do this are no longer in the running; they fell by the wayside because they did not fulfill that MSF.

7.4 The Success of the Minimum

As we have explained above, any market segment will usually have minimum success factors. But on a different note, the minimum has come into its own in recent years with the boom in low-cost strategies (although, rather than the minimum, low cost is more about the basics or the essentials of the market, as far as the needs to be satisfied are concerned). In fact, as we saw in Chapter 3, low cost is a strategy, not a KSF in a segment. No consumer appreciates the low cost of a company; the customer actually has no idea of the costs incurred by the company from which he makes purchases, nor indeed is he interested in them.

For the sake of clarity, we could say that the low-cost segment is the segment that values what it is offered by companies that follow this strategy. Specifically, these customers value very highly the price they are offered. Moreover, they are customers who nearly always forsake the market's KSFs and concentrate solely on the MSFs. They are even prepared to do some of the work that used to be done by the company, as we mentioned in Chapter 3.

This phenomenon is a very good example of the importance of analyzing the market, and also of its great dynamism (as is the case with all strategic perspectives). In recent years the low-cost phenomenon has created segments that did not exist previously, and has increased the importance of existing ones. The airline industry is paradigmatic in this respect. The low-cost segment has enabled many people who had never considered flying to do so, and others to fly much more than they used to. It has created new market space to a considerably greater extent than it has cannibalized other already existing segments.

Furthermore, it should be borne in mind that the same person can be in one segment when working (e.g. fly in business class for a business trip) but another when on holiday (fly in economy class with the family). To complicate matters still further, the same customer may combine segments. For example, he or she may fly with a low-cost company and stay at a five-star hotel; have lunch at a fast-food chain and dinner at a luxury restaurant; match a garment from Prada with one from Zara. The inexpensive, the low-cost, is no longer seen as shoddy and in bad taste, even by the upper classes.

The low-cost segment has also transformed the importance of some key success factors. For example, in some markets quality is no longer associated with price; the existing quality–price ratio has been overcome and consumers perceive price much more dynamically, accepting different prices depending on the moment and the channel.

Although low cost had already appeared and was here to stay prior to the crisis of 2007–2011, the crisis reaffirmed this segment still further. In the USA at the beginning of 2010 own-brand products were reaching 20 percent of the market. With regard to airlines, of all the air passengers who passed through Spain in the first six months of 2009, 51.7 percent (12.49 million people) did so with low-cost airlines. Low-cost airlines such as Ryanair (more than 65 million passengers) and EasyJet (more than 45 million passengers) were among the European leaders in 2009.

Obviously, this does not mean that all companies should target this type of segment, or even that they should target it in addition to others. All it means is that all companies should analyze this phenomenon in their market, what trend it is following, how it affects the company, and what the company should do about it as a result. The answer may be not to target this segment, but rather to react to it. Examples of this strategic path are provided by market leaders such as Danone, Kellogg's and Nestlé, among others. During 2009 they stated publicly through a major advertising campaign that they did not make own-brand products, with the slogan "it isn't the same". These manufacturers were stating that they were leaders in quality, innovation and trust, key success factors that they wanted to highlight in contrast to the low-cost segment.

Nevertheless, low cost does not always mean lack of differentiation. Some of the major internationally renowned manufacturers specializing in own-brand products may also have cutting-edge R&D, innovative products, and even high quality.[1] For its part, Mercadona, the most successful Spanish company with an own brand, states that its products actually do bear the identity of the producer and guarantees that its model is one of maximum quality. Logically, innovation can also happen in own brands in industries other than food, for example, Décathlon's "fitness cube" and its "2 seconds" tents.

The example of market-leading manufacturers standing up to own brands serves us as a reminder of the essential core of this market analysis. As was emphasized in Figure 7.1, the company must be acquainted with all the segments in its market and what is valued (KSFs and MSFs) in each of them. On the basis of this knowledge it must choose which segments to target. According to this decision, according to the segment or segments the company wants to target, it must satisfy the corresponding KSFs and MSFs. Consequently, it must build a strategy that matches, that satisfies, these factors.

We are continuing to complete the GIB model; we are continuing to gain strategic clarity by possessing more and more strategic perspectives

7.5 Questions for Reflection

I.   What variables are used to segment your market?

II. What segments does your market have?

   a. Segment

   b. Key success factors (KSFs) of the segment

   c. Minimum success factors (MSFs) of the segment

   d. Description of the segment at present

   Do this exercise as many times as segments you think your market may have (or if there are a very large number, as many as may be of interest to you).

III. What segments does your company target at present?

IV. Connection between market and industry: What strategic group targets each of these segments? In other words, what strategic dimensions match the KSFs and MSFs of each segment?[2]

   a. Segment/Strategic group

   b. KSFs and MSFs/Strategic dimensions

   Do this exercise as many times as there are segments targeted by your company.
      You could also extend this exercise to other segments not covered by your company, either because they may potentially be interesting in the future or in order to gain a better understanding of the competitive situation of your industry and market.

V.   What changes do you think will occur in the future in these segments? Set the time scale of your thinking bearing in mind the characteristics of your market:

   a. Segment

   b. Changes in the KSFs of the segment

   c. Changes in the MSFs of the segment

   d. Changes in its characteristics (number of customers, sales, margins, growth)

Do this exercise for all the segments described in the previous point that are liable to change in the future.

VI. What segments might be interesting for your company in the future?

    a. Segment

    b. KSFs of the segment

    c. MSFs of the segment

    d. Description (number of customers, sales, margins, growth)

    e. Strategic dimensions of the strategic group that targets the segment

    f. Competitors who form part of this strategic group

CHAPTER 8

Resources and Capabilities

In addition to being an outstanding painter, draughtsman and sculptor, Leonardo da Vinci conceived the helicopter, the parachute, the automobile and the submarine, among other things, more than 400 years ago. But he was never able to make them. He did not possess the resources and the capabilities to make them. A company can imagine the best of strategies, but if it does not have the resources and capabilities to put its strategic vision into practice that vision will lie dormant like those ideas of Leonardo's, until this company has sufficient resources and capabilities – or until some other firm that does have them catches on to the same strategy.

The analyses we have carried out so far have focused on the company's surroundings (macro analyses, the two levels of the industry, and the market), as we saw in Figure 7.1. In this chapter we will broach the internal analysis of the company. With the analyses performed up to now, a company can get a very clear idea of its competitive situation. It can know the strategic conditions of both its industry and its market, and the influence exerted on them by the macro environment. However, it will never be able to make a decision solely on the basis of this knowledge, as it lacks one part of what Kenichi Ohmae once described as the strategic triangle.[1]

This triangle neatly sums up the analyses made so far, with the addition of the analysis we are now embarking on: industry-market-company. All three are always influenced by the macro environment, as expressed in Figure 8.1. The industry tells us about the situation of the competitors (with regard to the company). The market tells us about customers' demands. And the inside of the company must tell us about the necessary resources and capabilities.

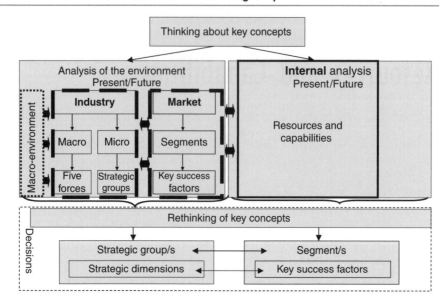

Figure 8.1 GIB model: Analyses we have carried out so far and their connection with the analysis of the company' resources

Therefore, another way of expressing the industry-market-company triangle is to replace it with their equivalents: competition-customer-resources. We could say that this strategic triangle should result in the company satisfying its customers' needs (market) better than its competitors (industry) by means of its resources and capabilities (inside).

In this chapter we will develop the hitherto unexplored angle of the triangle, that of resources and capabilities.

8.1 Key Result Areas

Before considering the core competences it must possess in order to carry out a strategy, the company should first engage in such a crucial exercise of strategic thinking as that concerning its resources. All companies stake their strategy on just a small number of areas, activities or departments, their key result areas (KRAs).[2] Only these areas, not all the company's areas, are essential. In other words, a company can afford not to be the best in all its areas (after all, who could be?), but it cannot afford not to be the best in its KRAs.

What are a company's KRAs? They are the areas responsible for carrying out its strategy, those that devise and are responsible for its strategic dimensions. Consequently, there are seldom many key areas in the company. There might even by just one. But usually we will find two or three areas; no more, because it is important to bear in mind that only those areas that are responsible for achieving the strategic dimensions that define the firm's strategy are KRAs.

In the previous chapter we mentioned that the company Audi carried out a strategy that had as its strategic dimensions high quality, technology, innovation and design, together with a brand image positioned in these dimensions, thus implying the recognition of high prestige. If these are its strategic dimensions, what will be the key areas? They should be R&D, responsible for quality, technology and innovation; design, on which this dimension depends; and marketing, the function of which is to achieve the brand awareness and positioning described above.

Audi cannot afford not to be competitive in R&D, design and marketing, because if it performs poorly in its KRAs it will be outperformed in them by its competitors. This will mean that these competitors with better R&D, design and marketing will overtake them in the strategic dimensions of quality, technology, innovation, design and brand image, the keys to its competitive position. And this is tantamount to saying that its competitors will perform the strategy better than it will.

If we think of Swatch watches, we could deduce that its strategic dimensions are basically an innovative design, a certain quality, a strong brand image, and low costs (in order to achieve a moderate price). In this case, the KRAs would be the R&D and engineering departments (responsible for design, quality and low cost) and the marketing department (responsible for its effective communication). As in any company, if Swatch underperforms in its KRAs it will not carry out its strategy to the same standard as its competitors, which always has dramatic consequences.

In short, no company can afford to have poorly performing KRAs; its KRAs must perform at least as well as those of its competitors, if not better. However, a company can afford to be less than outstanding in the remaining areas, those that are not KRAs. As we mentioned earlier, it is very difficult for an organization to do everything perfectly. In Chapter 10, which deals with the strategic perspective of the company's value chain, we will go deeper into the potentially major strategic consequences of the fact of a company having non-key areas and the decisions that may derive from it.

Another point that should be taken into account while on the subject of KRAs is that in view of the fact that all organizations have limited resources (each in relation to its size, logically), it would be advisable to focus on those aspects that are basic for their success. The organization should concentrate its efforts and its relatively scarce resources on the areas that

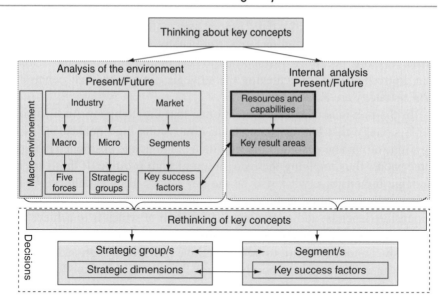

Figure 8.2 Addition of the analysis of key result areas to the GIB model

will bring it maximum benefits, as it is these that will have most influence on the factors that the market will value most.

Figure 8.2 presents the addition of a company's key result areas to the GIB model. As the KRAs are related to the company's strategy, to its strategic dimensions, and therefore to the key success factors that the company seeks to satisfy, it can be seen that the KRAs are connected to the KSFs. The nature of the KSFs that the company wishes to satisfy will dictate the nature of its KRAs.

8.2 Resources and Capabilities

It is important to be aware of the differences between resources and capabilities, and also to note the existence of two very distinct types of resources. It could be said that resources are the source, the components, the raw materials of capabilities. Conversely, capabilities can be seen as the outcome of the cooperation and coordination of resources, the result of how the firm uses and organizes its resources.

An organization possesses tangible resources, assets such as facilities or premises, vehicles, machinery, staff and funding. And it also has intangible, immaterial resources such as its reputation, brands, knowledge and information.

A company may have ample resources such as those described, yet may be unable to use them to develop correspondingly high capabilities. There is little sense in possessing great technologies, facilities, a highly renowned brand or a large sum of money if they cannot be used effectively. The opposite may also happen: a company without much in the way of resources, for example with less technology, facilities, brand and capital, may achieve substantial capabilities. Cooperation among the people in the organization and coordination among its resources maximize them; the management of these resources gets the most out of them.

The most important resources, those that nourish the core competences, those that lead to the achievement of competitive advantages, are the intangible ones. However, the tangible ones are the most visible, the most obvious. If we look at a company's balance sheet we will see mostly tangible assets (although in recent years the intangible ones have started to appear). If a balance sheet shows mainly tangible assets, the resulting image may be misleading as regards capabilities. Two companies might have similar balance sheets, with similar tangible resources, yet one of them might have almost no intangible resources whereas the other might possess a considerable reserve. The visible part of the resources is similar in the two cases, but while one company shows everything it has to show, the other conceals, like an iceberg in the ocean, a large amount of intangible resources that endow it with future possibilities that are unimaginable for the other organization.

The continuous development of knowledge, the acquisition of competences, experimentation, the dissemination of knowledge and the creation of a learning culture have been highlighted by several authors.[3] Ulrich actually went as far as to state a formula to measure the learning capabilities of an organization: **G** x **G**. The two **G**s in question were the ability to **G**enerate new ideas and the ability to **G**eneralize these new ideas. An organization that generates ideas but fails to generalize them does not develop. Neither does another that has the ability to disseminate them but is incapable of creating them. Both **G**s are indispensable.

The term "competences" is used to refer to the skills and abilities by which resources are deployed effectively through an organization's activities and processes.[4] In short, an organization's resources are important, but its capabilities, its ability to use those resources, are much more so, because capabilities maximize resources and therefore also the sources of competitive advantages.

8.3 Strategic Thinking about Capabilities

If we return to the strategic thinking process, from this perspective of capabilities, the first question the company has to ask itself is this: what capabilities are needed to carry out the strategy we want to implement?

These competences can be divided into five main categories:

Skills. The knowledge, the experience, the aptitude possessed by the people in an organization. In this category we can study in depth everything that is encompassed within the area of human resources. In this way we are adding the perspective of the human resource area to the strategic jigsaw puzzle we are piecing together by means of the GIB model (as we said earlier, all the areas of a company will appear). Therefore, the organization must ask itself what skills its staff must possess in order to carry out the strategy the company plans to implement.

Technology or know-how. Not all knowledge lies in the people who make up the organization. Here we would include such potentially important aspects as technology, patents, systems and databases. If we consider the areas of the company, here we would be adding to the GIB model those types of knowledge that are based on R&D, information systems and operations. Again, the strategic question from this capability is about what aspects related to technology or know-how it is necessary for the company to possess for it to be able to successfully carry out the strategy resulting from the thinking process.

Other intangibles. Not all intangibles have to do with the people in the organization or its technology or know-how. Intangibles such as a particular brand image and in-depth knowledge of that brand might be needed. Or the strategy might require a large market share offering a dominant position and the opportunity to have a close knowledge of the market. In connection with these other intangibles, the company must also ask itself what level of needs the pursued strategy demands.

Financial capabilities. This includes the capital owned by the company, the possibility of extending it, and its present and future borrowing capacity. Obviously, we can gain insight into this capability through knowledge of the area of finance. All strategies require a – sometimes very maximum – minimum of funding, and this may be a filter that the company cannot get through. As such, this issue must also be addressed when considering the necessary capabilities for implementing the strategy.

Other tangible assets. These derive from absolutely tangible assets such as the organization's facilities, premises, machinery, land and vehicles. As we have already mentioned, intangible assets are strategically much more important in most cases. However, this does not mean that on occasions physical assets may not pose an obstacle for putting a given strategy into practice. Hence the necessity to consider what demands the strategy imposes in this respect.

Therefore, from this capabilities perspective, the first strategic question the company has to ask itself is what human, technological, other intangible, financial and other tangible capabilities are required by the strategy concerned. In Figure 8.3 we add these issues to the GIB model.

This first addition of capabilities to the GIB model also implies a second strategic question: what capabilities does the company have at present? In fact, these two questions enable us to conclude wherein lies the difference between the company's present capabilities and the capabilities it needs to carry out the strategy it is thinking about. This is a key strategic result within the thinking process in which we are engaged.

However, these two questions, required capabilities versus the company's present competences, together with the strategic conclusion drawn

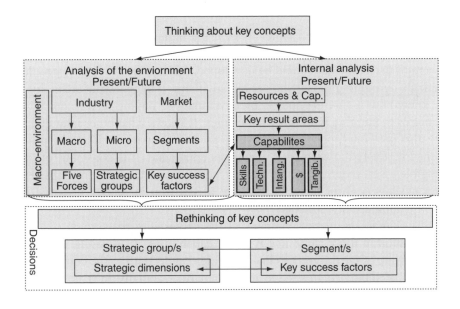

Figure 8.3 Addition of the analysis of the company's capabilities to the GIB model

from them, are not sufficient to see the full picture as regards capabilities. We need more information to know the real situation of the company when it comes to its capabilities and the strategy it is considering.

Right from the beginning of this book, it has been emphasized that strategy is a relative game: it is not about being good but about being better. We must satisfy our customers' needs better than our competitors do. Consequently, it will be of vital importance to know how our competitors – the companies in the industry who follow the same strategy that we want to apply – stand in relation to the core competences.

This raises a third question in this thinking about capabilities: what capabilities do our competitors possess? And as in the case of the same question about our own company, in comparison with the capabilities required to carry out the strategy, again we can draw a conclusion about the gap between our competitors' present capabilities and the capabilities they need.

In short, on the basis of the three strategic questions about capabilities (those that are needed, those the company now has, and those the competition now has), we obtain the two essential differences regarding capabilities: the capabilities the company lacks and those the competition lacks. Or to say the same thing differently, the capabilities that the company should develop if it wants to carry out this strategy and those the competition should deploy.

With this information under its belt, the organization now really does have a very clear idea of its situation with respect to its capabilities. It is aware of the skills that should be developed, perhaps by hiring new people, perhaps by training those who are already there. It knows what technology or know-how it should acquire, by developing it, buying it, forming joint ventures or merging with other companies. It knows what other intangibles are also necessary, possibly to develop the brand image so it can be positioned in a way the segment's customers appreciate. It is conscious of the tangible assets required by the strategy, perhaps new facilities, perhaps certain machinery. And lastly, it is aware of the sum of money involved in making all these investments.

The organization can compare all the above with the situation of the competition in those same five types of capabilities. As a result, it is perfectly aware of the differences in capabilities between it and the competition in each of them. At this stage the company is actually in a position to decide whether the strategy is feasible from this capabilities perspective, that is, whether the capabilities it must develop are attainable – always taking into account the situation of the competition as regards those same capabilities.

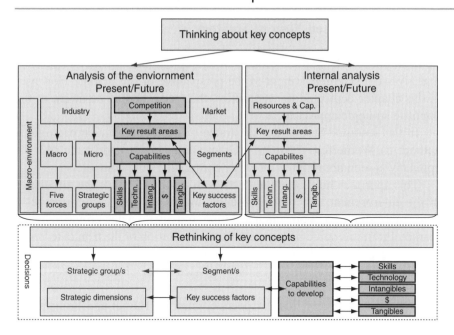

Figure 8.4 Addition of the analysis of the capabilities of the competition to the GIB model, and of the decisions derived from the analysis of capabilities: capabilities to develop

In Figure 8.4 we add the last two capability-related stages to the GIB model: the analysis of the capabilities of the competition and the final decision about the various capabilities that the company must develop in order to deploy the strategy.

It can be seen in the figure that, as in the case of the company itself, the KRAs of the competitors also interlink with the KSFs of the market they are targeting, since again the nature of these KSFs will dictate whether certain areas or others will be key. By definition, if they are competitors they will be targeting the same segment, thus having the same KRAs as the company.

In the analysis of the environment, the GIB model has already taken the competition into account. Competitors appeared in the micro industry analysis. But in that analysis they were studied in terms of the strategy they carried out; the description focused on the strategic dimensions they used and the strategic group or groups they belonged to. Now we have added the competition not for what it does (strategy) but for the capabilities it has. This analysis differs from and complements the one described earlier.

8.4 Resource-based View of Strategy

So far we have followed the process of strategic thinking with an approach that gives considerable weight to the perspective of the market. However, in this chapter dedicated to capabilities, the reader should be aware of the opposite strategic approach.

In this resource-based view of strategy, developed by such prestigious authors as Wernerfelt,[5,6] Quinn,[7] Grant[8] and Hamel and Prahalad,[9] the company is seen above all as an entity comprising core competences.

This approach holds that the key lies in resources, since the turbulence of the environment, its constant change, makes the firm's competences a much more stable basis on which to define strategy than that provided by the market. From this strategic perspective, the definition of the firm in terms of what it is capable of achieving, using its resources, can offer a much sturdier foundation for defining strategy than one based on the changing needs of the market.

A good example of this perspective, cited by Hamel and Prahalad, is the case of Honda. From its foundation in 1948 until today, this Japanese company has based its strategy on its ability to develop and manufacture engines, which has brought it to make a wide range of products in addition to motorcycles and cars, always incorporating an engine (e.g. lawnmowers, rotary tillers, chipper shredders, outboard motors, generators, pumps, snowblowers).

Therefore, this strategic view goes beyond using capabilities as a filter in the strategic process, enabling the firm to weigh up its feasibility, clarifying whether the firm will be capable of carrying out the strategy on the basis of the capabilities it can muster. This strategic view goes further inasmuch as it builds the strategy from the starting point of its capabilities, it bases the strategy on them, it seeks differentiation through them. The company works from the basis of the capabilities it masters better than the other companies in the industry.

In the closing chapters of this book we will return to this strategic view as part of the development of a new strategic model.

8.5 Questions for Reflection

I. Taking into account your company's strategy, what are its key result areas (activities or departments)?

II. What strategic dimension/s does each of these key areas perform?

III. What core competences are necessary in each of these key areas (in order to perform the strategic dimension/s better than the competition)?

   a. Skills

   b. Technology or know-how

   c. Other intangibles

   d. Financial capabilities

   e. Other tangible assets

IV. What capabilities does your company possess at present in each of these key areas? As a result, what is the difference between the required capabilities and those currently possessed by your company?

   a. Skills

   b. Technology or know-how

   c. Other intangibles

   d. Financial capabilities

   e. Other tangible assets

V. What capabilities does your competition possess at present in each of these key areas? As a result, what is the difference between the required capabilities and those currently possessed by your competition?

   a. Skills

   b. Technology or know-how

   c. Other intangibles

   d. Financial capabilities

   e. Other tangible assets

VI. In those capabilities in which it is necessary, how can your company enhance its capabilities in order to narrow the gaps detected?

VII. Repeat each of the six questions above, but instead of thinking about the present strategy of your company, think about the strategy it might consider pursuing in the future.

CHAPTER 9

Industry Value Chain

In 2010, farmers all over the world marched, not for the first time, in protest against the low prices they received for their products. The crop and livestock industries complained that they sold almost at cost price, sometimes even below it, whereas the price paid by the end consumer was usually several times the sum they received.

By way of example of the thousands of demonstrations that took place during 2010, we could mention those in July in Brussels in front of the seat of the European Union by dairy farmers protesting that the production cost of milk was higher than their selling price; those in Belgrade in June claiming that the sale price of wheat covered only half their costs; those that took place in April in which French grain farmers converged on Paris demanding urgent government action to boost prices to counter sharp falls in income in the past two years; and those in Madrid in May in which livestock farmers denounced "the abusive practices of some distribution companies". In May cotton farmers in Zimbabwe even refused to harvest the crop in protest against the low prices being offered on the local market. Just an account of these innumerable protests, which continued well after the period described here, would in itself fill a book.

To analyze the reasons for this problem affecting farmers, in order to understand how it was possible for them to receive so little when the end consumer sometimes paid so much, we need to take a look at the industry value chain.

9.1 Description

So far in the GIB model we have analyzed the industry from two perspectives: the macro, through the five competitive forces, and the micro,

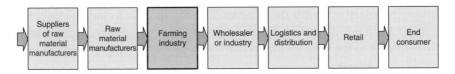

Figure 9.1 Simplified example of the farming industry value chain

with strategic groups. Industry value chain analysis views the industry even more widely than the macro analysis.[1] The macro analysis encompassed the industry's suppliers and customers (together with possible new entries and substitutes), whereas the value chain broadens this view: it stretches from the beginning to the end of the chain. In this way, the industry value chain starts with the first industry that supplies it with some component or raw material and finalizes with the end consumer. Thus the view afforded by the macro analysis is extended in both directions.

The first strategic question from this industry value chain perspective is precisely about how to put together the chain itself, how to think about it. We could word it as follows: What is the value chain of our industry? For example, if we are considering the value chain of the crop or livestock farming industry, we could depict it as shown in abbreviated form in Figure 9.1.

The chain could start with some manufacturer of raw materials, such as fertilizer or animal feed, depending on whether we are dealing with a crop or livestock farm. In fact, the component manufacturer would in turn have various other suppliers (still more links in the chain). However, we present this value chain in reduced form, without specifying the previous links in any detail, as our intention is merely illustrative.

The farming industry could sell its products to a wholesaler or an industrial company which will process its products in some way (for example, a meat processing firm or a company that produces fruit in syrup). Or it could sell its products directly to a distribution or retail firm, in this case chains of hypermarkets, "horeca" (hotels, restaurants and catering) or specialist stores, although the great majority of sales occur through hypermarkets.

Clearly all these links in the chain do not always exist. For example, a producer might sell directly to a chain of supermarkets, in which case the intermediate links do not exist.

9.2 Distributing Value

It is worth bearing in mind that we are describing a concept called the industry value chain: "industry" and "chain" because it is made up of a series of industries placed one after the other to form the links of a chain, although it is also true that it is looking increasingly like a value network rather than a chain, owing to the ever greater possibilities of relationship and connection between these links.

And we include the word "value" precisely because each link, each industry, must add value. If one of the industries fails to add value to the chain, it is signing its own death warrant. It will disappear without any doubt whatsoever; all that remains to be known is the exact date on which this painful sentence is to be carried out.

As a result, the second strategic question to ask from this industry value chain perspective is how the value is shared out among the industries that make up the chain. In other words, if the end consumer pays 100, we need to know how that 100 is distributed among all the industries that form the chain. Figure 9.2 shows a graphic representation of this strategic question.

If we think about this vital question in the case of the protesting farmers in 2010, we will see their problem depicted in the figure. In the distribution of value, their industry must have got to keep only a small proportion, an insufficient amount to cover their costs and provide a reasonable margin. In some cases the price paid by the consumer (that final 100) might be so low that all the industries in the chain will feel the pinch. But to judge by the statements made by those concerned, the first option seems to be much more common.

Consequently, the fact that these protesting farmers did not dominate the value chain led them to occupy a weak position in relation to the rest of the industries that belonged to it – or simply in relation to one of them, because the existence of one industry in the chain imposing its power can be enough. For example, some demonstrators stated that they sold 80 percent of their production to superstores, which then set whatever prices they wanted, and that they were forced to accept these prices unless they wanted to run the risk of not selling their products. The factors of bargaining power we saw in Chapter 5 clearly account for this situation.

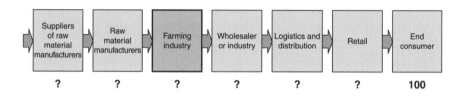

Figure 9.2 Example of an approach to the strategic question of value distribution applied to the example of the farming industry value chain

In the context of this second strategic perspective of the industry value chain, an industry may perceive a decreasing value, a tendency for the amount it receives to decrease over the years. This may be because other industries dominate the chain, as seems to happen sometimes with farm produce. Or it may be for an even more serious reason: the aforementioned inability of the industry to add value.

Think of the wholesalers in any industry. One day the retailers to whom they sell might decide to club together and form purchasing groups that start to perform the functions that until then had been performed by the wholesalers. At that time, that wholesaler industry should start to understand that its time will soon be up, as it no longer provides its customers with value. This is one of the possible strategic conclusions that can be drawn from analyzing the industry value chain: we might find that the industry is nearing its end – which, although tragic, is always better to discover sooner and firsthand than later and from someone else. In this way the companies in the industry can pull out of it in an orderly fashion and without the losses caused by discovering that one is no longer competitive on the evidence of a prolonged succession of large sums in red on the balance sheet.

9.3 Changing Value

So far we have thought about the situation as it stands: the nature of the industry value chain and how value is distributed among its industries. Now we shall move on and consider how the value possessed by an industry can be changed, or discover that this is not possible.

There are two possible ways of bringing about this change of value within a chain, or in other words, of trying to increase the value of one's own industry (as seemed to be the case of the farmers).

9.3.1 Vertical Integration

The first way is by means of vertical integration. If we observe that one of the links/industries is appropriating a large proportion of the value, there is the option of performing the function of this industry and thus appropriating its value.

Five fishermen's associations in the Spanish province of Girona, Spain (Llançà, L'Escala, Palamós, Sant Feliu de Guíxols and Blanes) created Giropesca in 2004 (although it did not start to operate until 2005), on finding that the distribution of the value in their industry chain was unfavorable

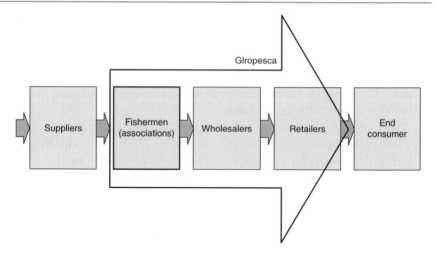

Figure 9.3 Vertical integration as a way of changing value in the industry value chain: the case of Giropesca

to them, as wholesalers and retailers held a large part of the value. The function of this new company was to participate in the distribution process, that is, in selling their catch, integrating forwards and performing the functions of wholesaler and retailer, as depicted in Figure 9.3.

If an industry is integrated and performs the functions of other industries in its chain, as in this case, with fishermen performing the functions of wholesalers and retailers, it can distribute the value among the industries in which it participates as it wishes. In effect it has appropriated the value of these industries, as in fact it now forms part of them.

However, this involves potential risks. In an integration initiative, the company or industry concerned becomes a competitor of its customers if it integrates forwards, as in the case of Giropesca.[2] Therefore, it runs the risk of causing an adverse reaction from its customers. In the summer of 2005, when Giropesca started to operate, the wholesalers' and retailers' associations reacted by ceasing to purchase fish in the markets belonging to those fishermen's associations. They accused the fishermen of unfair competition, even going so far as to announce that they would take the case to the Competition Tribunal. This proved unnecessary, as in the face of this reaction Giropesca abandoned the project.

Of course, this is not to say that all integration initiatives end this way. Without even leaving this same industry, we find examples of shipowners that have opened fishmonger's shops and have agreements with restaurants. There are also other fishermen's associations that have gone down the same road as Giropesca. Not to mention the numerous production industries, including farming, that contact the consumer directly.

On a different note, sometimes after performing an integration initiative a strategic decision is made to pull out of one of the industries. La Sirena is Spain's leading frozen food retail group and has been for years. In the past the company manufactured around 20 percent of the goods it sold, but following its purchase from Agrolimen by the investment fund 3i in 2006, it gave up manufacturing to become essentially a firm specializing in the distribution of frozen food.

9.3.2 Bypassing A Link/Industry

The second way of bringing about a change of value within a chain, that is, of increasing the value of a company or an industry, is much better than the first. In integration, the industry or firm appropriated value by performing the function of the supplier or customer industry. In this second option, the firm or industry retains the value of the supplier or customer industry without even performing its function. This is why this second way is even better than the first.

However, this way of changing value imposes a demand: the industry to be bypassed is consequently going to disappear, since it does not provide its customers – or at least some of them – with value.

The Dell business model started up from this perspective. In 1984 Michael Dell thought that there were customers for whom computer stores provided very little value, and who would therefore be willing to act as stores themselves, performing the functions usually performed by the store: to look at a variety of computers or specifications, choose each characteristic and so design their computer. Thus, if an industry drops out of the chain (as was the case of computer retail stores in the Dell model), the company appropriates the value of distribution without even performing its functions.

The advent of low-cost airlines was based on this same intuition, namely that for some consumers travel agencies provided very little value. What function are we performing when we enter a website and look up different flight times, airlines and prices for a trip we have to take? What are we continuing to do when we choose a particular time, airline and price, when we pay for it, and even when we book a seat on the plane? We are performing the function of the travel agency. The airline concerned has appropriated the value once possessed by the travel agency without even having to perform its functions, because they are being performed by the customer, the end consumer.

As we mentioned in Chapter 3, this phenomenon of the end customer performing functions that used to be performed by an industry is one of the ways in which companies that follow a low-cost strategy achieve their objectives. From this industry value chain perspective we gain a much better understanding of their logic.

In these cases where a company or an industry – the first step tends to be taken by a company, the rest of the industry then following suit – bypasses one of the industries that form part of the chain, it must ask itself a strategic question: what share of the appropriated value (previously belonging to the "bypassed" industry) it should give to the customer and what share the company should keep. This question is highly strategic, because the greater the portion of value given to the customer, usually in the form of lower price, the more attractive the resulting model will be.

Figure 9.4 shows the addition of this industry value chain view to the GIB model.

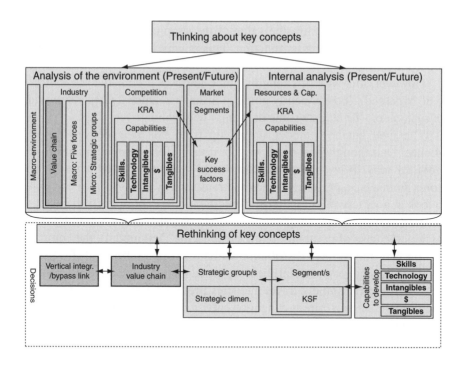

Figure 9.4 Addition of industry value chain analysis, and the decisions derived from it, to the GIB model

As can be seen in the figure, the industry analysis is enlarged with a third perspective: industry value chain analysis. This requires the company to make further strategic decisions with the aim of acquiring more value from its chain: the possibility of vertical integration or the potential bypassing of an industry in the chain.

Equally, this figure highlights that all the strategic decisions to be taken as a result of the thinking process are interconnected. Each one influences all the others. We mentioned at the beginning of the development of the GIB model that, as we add concepts, pieces in the strategic jigsaw puzzle that we are putting together, we gain increasing strategic clarity; our understanding of the competitive situation improves. Decisions can only be made once the whole thinking process is complete, once all the strategic concepts and perspectives involved in this process are known.

Each piece in the strategic jigsaw puzzle clearly influences the rest of the pieces, as all the strategic concepts are undeniably interrelated. This phenomenon is maintained right through until the last stage of the GIB model.

9.4 Questions for Reflection

I. What is the value chain of your industry? Describe its links/industries until you reach the end consumer.

II. How is the value distributed among each of the industries that make up the chain?

III. With the aim of changing this value distribution with a view to your industry/company obtaining a larger proportion, might it be of interest to carry out vertical integration?

IV. With the aim of changing this value distribution with a view to your industry/company obtaining a larger proportion, might it be possible to bypass one of the links or industries in the chain?

V. Is your industry/company threatened by the prospect of other industries integrating and penetrating your industry?

VI. Is your industry/company threatened with being bypassed by other industries in your chain?

VII. Does the above thinking require any strategic change from your company?

VIII. Ask yourself the above questions again, this time thinking about the situation of your industry value chain in the mid- and/or long term (the period of time you consider to be reasonable for this type of thinking given the characteristics of your industry).

CHAPTER 10

Company Value Chain

Usain Bolt smashed the 100-meter world record several times in 2008 and 2009 with extraordinary and blatant superiority. He also held the world records for the 200-meters and the 4×100-meters relay. He was three times Olympic champion (in these same events) in Beijing 2008, as well as world champion in these three events in Berlin 2009. This incredible Jamaican athlete achieved all these astounding records and gold medals running in shoes made by the firm Puma.

However, despite the fact that Bolt ran with Puma, Nike continued to dominate the worldwide sportswear (shoes, clothing and gear) industry in 2008 and 2009, as it had in previous years. Why did Nike enjoy that 'Bolt type' superiority in those years? Why were other companies in the industry such as Adidas, Reebok, Asics, Mizuno and indeed Bolt's Puma unable to topple the Oregon firm from its position of global leadership during those years? Was Nike so superior? Did it master all aspects of its business? Did it want to master them? Was it crucial to its strategy that some of its activities (such as manufacturing) were outsourced? How can one arrive at the conclusion that the outsourcing of an activity is desirable?

In order to be able to answer these questions accurately we need another analysis, a new strategic perspective, to complement those we already have; an analysis that starts with the pieces of the strategic jigsaw puzzle formed by the GIB model as it now stands (see Figure 9.4) and goes on to delve still further into internal aspects of a company's strategy: in short, company value chain analysis.

10.1 Description

The concept of the company value chain was first defined by the consultancy firm McKinsey, with the name 'business system'.[1] in 1980. It was designed by this firm to combine the concepts of competitive advantage and the decisions a company has to make within its organization as a consequence of that advantage.

In 1985, Michael Porter introduced the concept of the value chain on the basis of McKinsey's idea of the business system, popularising it enormously with his successful books and celebrated papers.[2] Because of this, we will start this chapter by describing the company value chain as Porter described it.

The idea of the company value chain is the same one as we saw in the previous chapter in connection with the industry, but here applied, of course, to the organization. In the previous chapter we established that each industry is a succession of sectors, each of them contributing value (otherwise the industry will disappear). In the case of the company, rather than a succession of industries we are dealing with a succession of activities, functions or departments, which again must provide value. This is the idea of the value chain as applied to the company.

In Figure 10.1 we present the division of the firm's activities into two groups: primary and support activities as M. Porter also pointed out. Primary activities are those that are in direct contact with the product or service. Therefore, they are the activities involved in its physical creation, its transport, its sale and its after-sales service. As a result they comprise R & D, purchases, logistics (inbound and outbound), operations, marketing, sales, distribution and service.

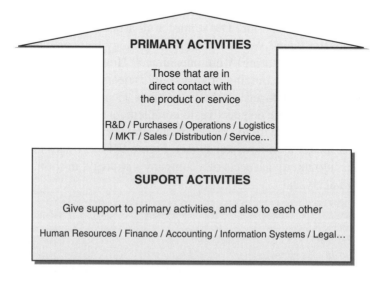

Figure 10.1   The two kinds of the firm's activities

Support activities, as their name indicates, give support to primary activities, and also to each other. They provide primary activities the indispensable human resources (HR management), finance, accounting, information systems, legal support and so on. All the support activities can sustain each and every one of the primary activities. For example, people are needed in all primary activities.

Logically, each of these activities can be subdivided still further if this is considered to be advisable for a better thinking process, since in fact they are made up of a variety of subactivities. Thus, for example, operations could be split into component manufacturing, processing, packing and quality control.

Although Porter's diagram is the one most commonly used in connection with the company value chain, a simpler presentation, closer to the diagram shown in the case of the industry value chain, would aid understanding of the various thinking processes that can be carried out on the basis of this tool, and to which the following sections will be dedicated.

For this reason, we prefer a presentation such as that shown in Figures 10.2 and 10.3. Furthermore, this diagram is closer to McKinsey's initial conception of the business system.

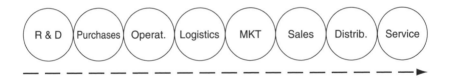

Figure 10.2 Company value chain: primary activities

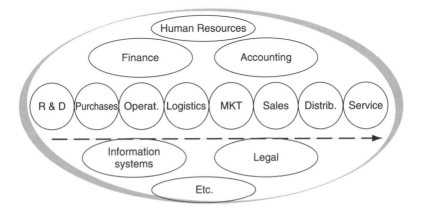

Figure 10.3 Company value chain

Figure 10.2 shows only the primary activities of the company value chain. However, Figure 10.3 shows all the activities in the chain, including support activities.

10.2 Core Activities

The first essential strategic question to pose from this company value chain perspective should lead us to conclude which of the activities performed by the company are core. This is a vital matter, because as we mentioned in connection with resources and capabilities in Chapter 8, the key areas of the company are very few. In fact, the core activities are the same as the key result areas (KRAs) described in that chapter. Now, with this change of strategic perspective, we call them core activities, but they are none other than those same KRAs.[3]

The reader will recall that it was essential to know these core activities, as the realization of the firm's strategy depended on them. This strategy was based on very few activities, not all of them. If we think of the case of Nike, discussed at the beginning of this chapter, what activities does it base its strategy on? If we establish that Nike's strategy is mainly about design and brand, not without a certain amount of technology, we will agree that its core activities will be R&D, design and marketing. Nike cannot afford not to be competitive in them. If it does not perform these functions well, it will not achieve its strategy.

This is why this first conclusion is so fundamental from this perspective. It is true that we already knew this conclusion (as KRAs), but it is also true that from this company value chain view it will lead us to further conclusions that we have not yet reached.

10.3 Strategy at the Level of Each Activity

So far we have thought about the strategy of the company with great precision. In Chapter 6 we looked at the strategy of the company in terms of the strategic dimensions that it seeks to achieve. This company value chain perspective triggers an additional and complementary question about company strategy: What strategy do we seek to achieve in each of the company's activities? This thinking leads to functional strategies, as an activity is none other than a functional area. Consequently, here the company asks itself about the strategy it seeks to achieve in R&D, purchases, operations, logistics, marketing, human resources, information systems and so on. It questions itself about the functional strategy of all the activities it carries out.

Of course, this strategy will be very different according to the activity, as each functional area has its own strategy. There will even be cases of very different – almost conflicting – strategies, since in some activities the priority will be to add value, to differentiate itself as much as possible, whereas in others the goal to achieve will be low cost, the reduction of costs. Obviously, these functional strategies will be very different, but they will always fit into the business strategy defined by the strategic dimensions that the company wishes to attain.

By getting to know strategy at the level of each activity, we gain a complementary, more precise definition of company strategy; we can understand it in greater depth. But in addition, this thinking about the firm's strategy in each of its activities brings us to another strategic question: Does the company achieve the strategy it has set itself in each of its activities (better than its competitors do)?

Logically, the answer to this question cannot always be yes. It is very difficult for a company to be the best in all the activities it carries out. Who is capable of being best at everything? Michael Jordan was one of the best basketball players of all time, if not the best. However, when he retired from basketball, still in full possession of his incredible skills, and took up baseball, he discovered that he couldn't be best at everything (and so returned to the sport in which he was king). Can a company be the best at R&D, purchases, operations, logistics, marketing, sales, distribution, service, human resources, information systems and everything else? Common sense tells us that it cannot, and this common sense is usually backed up by the facts.

Therefore, combining the three questions we have thought about so far from this company value chain perspective (whether or not the activity is core, the nature of the strategy in each area, and the extent to which the desired strategy is achieved in each function), we can get four possible types of answers. By considering whether or not the activity is core and whether or not the strategy is achieved, we get four strategic possibilities, as shown in Figure 10.4:

- Core activity that achieves the desired strategy

- Non-core activity that achieves the desired strategy

- Core activity that does not achieve the desired strategy

- Non-core activity that does not achieve the desired strategy

	Strategy achieved	Strategy NOT achieved
Core activities		
NON-core activities		

Figure 10.4 Summary table of the first three strategic questions about the company value chain

If we think about the two possibilities that involve core activities:

- Core activity that achieves the desired strategy: Company management will be highly satisfied. It's all plain sailing – at least from this company value chain perspective. Their only worry might be that success could go to the management team's head. This possibility should be dispelled as soon as they think about the absolute turmoil that reigns in any industry, meaning that strategic conclusions could cease to be valid at any moment. In short, this is the possibility in which all the company's core activities should find themselves.

- Core activity that does not achieve the desired strategy: An extremely serious strategic problem. In fact, no core activity can afford to be in this invidious box. If an activity does not achieve its strategy, by definition the firm's strategy will fail. So the company only has two possibilities: either it gets this activity to achieve the desired strategy very quickly or it has to change strategy. If the organization is aware that it cannot be the best in its industry at this core activity, that it cannot perform it better than (or at least as well as) the competitors that are seeking to achieve that same strategy, those same strategic dimensions, then it should abandon this strategy. If it does not, all it will achieve is to continue spending resources and ultimately fail to reach the desired strategic objective. In the case of Nike, if we have established that its core activities were R&D, design and marketing, it cannot afford any of these three functions to be in the dreaded unachieved core activity box.

Figure 10.5 sums up these conclusions with regard to the two core activity boxes, indicating the only possible ways forward in the event of a core activity not achieving its strategy.

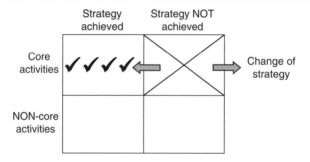

Figure 10.5 Summary table of the first three strategic questions about the company value chain, indicating the conclusions and possible solutions for the two core activity boxes

10.4 Outsourcing as a Strategic Possibility

If we think about the remaining two possibilities, those that involve non-core activities:

■ Non-core activity that achieves the desired strategy: It is very positive for any activity to get what it wants to achieve, to carry out the strategy of its function well; the people engaged in this activity work day after day to this end. Although it is not as vital as in the case of core activities, it is always satisfying when an area carries out its strategy well.

■ Non-core activity that does not achieve the desired strategy: Reverse reading from the previous box. It would be desirable to get this activity to carry out its strategy, but not achieving is not an exceptionally serious situation, as it was with unachieved core activities. In this case, the future of the strategy is not at stake; therefore neither is the future of the company. Furthermore, as we have already discussed, to some extent this situation is only to be expected, given the practical impossibility of a company being the best at everything it does.

These two reflections on non-core activities, especially the latter, lead to a third one. If a company does not achieve the desired strategy in a non-core activity, if it does not manage to master that activity and that function is not essential for its strategy, it can consider the possibility of not carrying it out. A company can ask itself whether it is good for it to carry out a non-core activity for which it does not possess competences, which it does not perform well. In fact, this question can even be asked about non-core

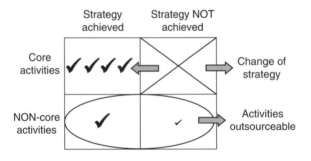

Figure 10.6 Summary table of the first three strategic questions about the company value chain, completed with the addition of the conclusions for the two non-core activity boxes

activities that it performs well; they too are outsourceable, especially if they are functions that add little value, that do not provide the company with a large margin.

Figure 10.6 sums up the conclusions with regard to the two non-core activity boxes, indicating that they are outsourceable. It must be stressed that in these non-core activities outsourcing is only a possibility. As we will see presently, sometimes it can be a big mistake to outsource a non-core activity.

All the analyses and tools we are developing as we build the GIB model are only a means to provoke thought; they never impose decisions. They question strategically; they do not impose strategic solutions. No tool for analysis, no concept, solves a strategic problem. It simply helps us to think about it. It is always the manager who has to decide. And as we know, this is no easy task, since all the perspectives involved in the GIB model are interrelated with each other.

Going back to the example of Nike, operations is not a core activity for this US firm. Therefore, as a function it is outsourceable. This would also be true for the Swatch Group, for example, as its strategy combines (depending on the type of watch and the segment it is aimed at) very different degrees of quality, design, technology, innovation, channel and brand image, sometimes together with low costs.[4] Consequently, in the case of Nike, operations is not a core activity, as it is not at the root of any of these strategic dimensions. However, Swatch is the biggest watchmaker in the world, with 156 production centers. Not only does this Swiss firm make and assemble all the models sold under its 19 brands, but it supplies the rest of the watch industry with parts. This is so because it could never consider the possibility of outsourcing production, as the potential manufacturers for outsourcing were in competition with it.

With Swatch the possibility of outsourcing was competitively unviable. Furthermore, not only did the firm have no choice but to assemble its own watches; it even had to make the parts, as its suppliers were also its competitors. In this case, the strategic option presented in Figure 10.6 was actually not an option at all. The company's strategic movement had to be away from outsourcing (ceasing to carry out one or more activities): vertical integration (adding new activities). Taking this obligation as a starting point, the company can try to build an additional advantage, attempt to become an expert in these functions, do them better than anybody else, and achieve a cost advantage in these functions in terms of both size (economies of scale) and accumulated experience. Today the vertical integration of the Swatch Group gives it both these competitive advantages.

In the event of it being competitively possible to outsource non-core activities, a company should weigh up the advantages and disadvantages that this strategic option will bring.

10.4.1 Advantages

Ceasing to carry out a function involves **less cost, investment, personnel and bureaucracy**, to a greater or lesser extent depending on the activity concerned. If operations is outsourced, this saving in cost, investment, personnel and bureaucracy is huge. If Nike made all the sportswear it sells, its structure would change enormously. In fact, outsourcing turns costs that used to be fixed (e.g. overheads, equipment, employees) into variable costs, as they are fixed for the outsourcee.

So, by outsourcing, the company makes a cost saving through which it has the possibility of **investing more resources in core activities**. And therefore these core activities – in which, we should remember, strategy must be achieved – now stand a greater chance of being done better. If Nike does not carry out the activity of operations, the huge savings in factories, employees, equipment and so on can be invested in R&D, design or marketing, activities in which its strategy really is at stake.

With part of the savings generated by outsourcing operations, in the future Nike might perhaps try to strike a sponsorship deal with Usain Bolt or some other sports star to balance out the advantage that Puma is achieving for its brand image (key dimension) in athletics by sponsoring this superathlete. Nike spends huge amounts of money by having on its payroll sports stars such as Rafael Nadal in tennis, LeBron James, Kobe Bryan and Pau Gasol in basketball, Andrés Iniesta and Cristiano Ronaldo in football (as Adidas does with Leo Messi, Xavi Hernández and David Villa); and whole teams such as FC Barcelona and Manchester United (just as Adidas does with Real Madrid). Nike might not be able to invest so much money on marketing (or design) if it had to make its own boots, running shoes or sportswear.

The third advantage of outsourcing arises when we ask ourselves about what sort of company to outsource an activity to. It will be a company for which that area is key, an organization that masters that function completely. Therefore, the third advantage of outsourcing is that **the outsourced activity is performed better**. The companies that manufacture for Nike perform this production to all the extremely high standards that this brand demands of them, as well as having competitive prices. They achieve this because they are companies for which operations is their core activity. Firms specializing in operations exist in the textile, pharmaceutical, construction, chemical, food, electronic and a good many other industries. For these firms, operations is a key area, whereas for the rest of the companies in their industries they are an outsourceable activity.

10.4.2 Disadvantages

However, like all strategic options, outsourcing also has **disadvantages**. To begin with, outsourcing means that the company ceases to perform one of its activities, so **it relinquishes the capabilities it possessed in the outsourced activity**. If at a later date the organization decides to perform that activity again, it will have to start building the necessary capabilities from scratch, with the great difficulties that this entails. This disadvantage is serious enough for the matter to warrant in-depth consideration before any decision is made – all the more so when the decision is irreversible.

Furthermore, **it is not easy to find a company to outsource an activity to** without some friction occurring. **Culture** compatibility problems may arise between the two companies. Or there may be difficulties in understanding the required **needs** and specificities. Or the **prestige** of the firm may be affected by the behavior of the outsourcee; the reader will recall the accusations of child labor or worker exploitation in some factories. Lack of **loyalty** may appear in the course of the relationship; for example, the firm might discover that its products have been copied and sold through parallel channels or under other brands. Or the outsourcee might not have the required future **capability** to perform. Of course, a company can outsource manufacturing and keep quality control, or outsource to more than one company, but it always loses competences in the outsourced activity, and these potential threats can always arise.

In view of all the above, it is a matter of finding a partner rather than a supplier; **it is a long-term relationship**. It is a relationship of trust, in which **confidential information can be conveyed**; in which control over an activity is lost, no matter how non-core it is. In addition, **company staff** affected by the outsourcing **may become demoralized**. There may even be a certain amount of unease among the rest of the staff, who may interpret this outsourcing as a first step toward further staff reductions. For this reason the move must be very well explained internally, although the risk of misunderstanding is always there.

Aspects that the company should assess when thinking about the appropriateness or otherwise of outsourcing a non-core activity can include whether it is a function that makes intensive use of resources, whether it is very dependent on other areas of the firm, whether its volume of work fluctuates much, whether it has to meet high standards, whether it is subject to extreme changes in demand, whether its staff is highly skilled, costly or difficult to find, or whether it has a technology that requires major investments. These are issues that, together with the advantages and disadvantages described above, help us to see more clearly the appropriateness or otherwise of the possible outsourcing of a non-core activity.

Figure 10.7 presents the addition to the GIB model of the three new strategic perspectives that the company value chain has contributed so far: knowledge of core activities, the strategy we seek to achieve in each activity, and the possible outsourcing of an activity.

As we can see in Figure 10.7, company value chain analysis and the various analyses derived from it appear in the internal analysis of the company as additional to the analysis we have considered up to now (resources and capabilities). It can also be seen in this figure that, in the decision section, those decisions we made up to now are likewise complemented with those resulting from thinking about the company value chain. These decisions are entirely dependent on the rest, as is expressed by the two-way arrows. We are continuing to complete the strategic jigsaw puzzle that is being developed through the GIB model.

However, the company value chain provides us with still more strategic perspectives; it is capable of causing still more thought processes with the aim of making new essential decisions.

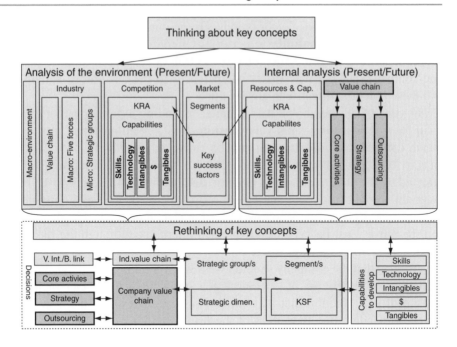

Figure 10.7 Addition to the GIB model of the first three strategic perspectives of company value chain analysis

10.5 Cooperation as a Way of Enhancing Activities

When discussing the various possible situations of the company's activities (see Figure 10.6), we concluded core activities should always be successfully carried out (or else the strategy should be rejected and another one sought for which this activity is not core), and also that non-core activities are potentially outsourceable, especially if they have not been successfully carried out so far.

We shall now introduce another possibility for enhancing an activity (whether or not it is core): cooperation, either internal (between activities within the same company) or external (between an activity in one company and another activity in another company). However, external cooperation is problematical when the activity is core.

Internal cooperation is based on enhancing the company's activities through collaboration, by sharing information and needs, and through team-work by the management and staff of the company's different departments. The various chapters of this book, the development of the GIB model, each of the analyses, decisions and concepts of which it is comprised, have left no room for doubt about the clear interrelationship that exists between all the areas of an organization.

Obviously, the more collaboration and teamwork there is between these functions, the better each function will be. Without marketing we cannot know what the customer really values. Without R&D and design we cannot innovate, we cannot satisfy that need felt by the customer better than the competition does. Without operations we cannot provide the product or service exactly as it was designed, or with the required quality and cost. Without purchases we do not have the vital components at the best price. Likewise, without human resources we do not have the most qualified personnel in each area. Without finance nothing is possible, because funding is vital for everything. And without distribution we do not reach the customer. We could carry on this reasoning with the rest of the areas. Every activity is important. Each of them depends on the rest. Each of them improves by being in contact with the rest, especially with those that have most influence on its decisions. In fact, in some areas there are decisions that require knowledge that lies in other functions.

This way of enhancing a company's activities is sometimes not exploited as fully as it could and should be. For this reason, teamwork and interdepartmental collaboration, ad hoc teams, interdepartmental projects, are essential in any organization.

In the course of a strategic thinking process open to managers of all the areas of a company, there is an obvious and expected end result of the process: their decisions. However, this is not the only big advantage for the organization of having engaged in a thinking process. One extremely important consequence of this process is the fact that each of the managers understands that his or her area is a vital part of the whole, a part that is interconnected with the rest of the company's areas. This in turn increases teamwork and interdepartmental collaboration, which as we have said are essential.

For its part, **external cooperation** can take several forms:

Strategic alliances. One-off agreements between companies to perform a particular activity, such as doing joint research or penetrating a country. For example, in July 2009 the Japanese Mitsubishi Corporation and the Spanish group Acciona constituted a strategic alliance to invest in renewables, both companies investing €2000 million in the joint development and exploitation of a wide range of renewable energy projects all over the world over the following three years. Their aim was to lead global development in renewable energies. They also included the possibility of analyzing joint business opportunities in water management and treatment and sustainable construction and transport.

Joint ventures. Formation of a new company by the companies participating in the cooperation, in order for this new company to perform the joint activity concerned. For example, in August 2009 PRISA (the leading media group in the Spanish and Portuguese-speaking markets) and IBN (InStore Broadcasting Network) announced a joint venture to introduce the retail media business into Spain, Portugal and Latin America. PRISA contributed its experience in radio programming, adapted to different markets, its news production capability and editorial experience, and its audiovisual production. IBN contributed its patented personalized in-store communication technology, with which it supplies US supermarket and pharmacy chains with music and interactive videos.

Mergers. The companies participating in the agreement disappear to form a new one in which the capital is distributed as agreed, usually without either of them holding a dominant position, since otherwise the operation would be more akin to an acquisition than to a merger. In Chapter 3 note 1 above we gave the example of the merger between Guinness PLC and Grand Metropolitan PLC to form Diageo PLC, which created the world's leading premium beverage corporation. We could also mention the merger between Fujitsu and Toshiba's cell phone businesses in October 2010 to create Japan's second largest mobile device manufacturer, by way of illustration that sometimes it is possible to merge only certain businesses instead of the whole company.

Acquisitions. One organization 'swallows' another or others, which disappear to become part of the buyer. We could cite the takeover of the mythical superhero factory Marvel (Spider-Man, X-Men) by Walt Disney for $4000 million in September 2009. The operation caused an earthquake in the entertainment industry – and gave Disney almost 5000 new characters, thus providing clear growth opportunities. It also balanced Mickey Mouse's firm demographically, as Disney's main box-office hits until then had appealed mostly to the female population, whereas Marvel offered products for very male tastes.

As can be seen through the examples given above, in all these forms of cooperation the idea is for the sum of the efforts of each company to result in a greater amount than what each one contributes separately. That is, $2 + 2$ should equal 7, and if possible 9, but at least 5. Or in other words, by collaborating, each company should obtain what it could not achieve on its own, in isolation.

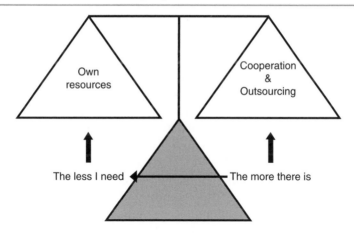

Figure 10.8 Balance of resources, or the impact of cooperation and outsourcing on the need for resources in an organization

This is fundamental today, when the resources of all organizations are limited, when all management teams are aware that they need better personnel, more knowledge and technology, and a higher market position and brand image; that they need to increase their financial capacity and/or improve their facilities. In fact, practicing cooperation means increasing one's strategic possibilities with the same resources. Outsourcing also has this effect: it extends the company's strategic possibilities without the need to increase resources.

We could imagine a balance of resources of the organization, as shown in Figure 10.8. On one side lie the company's resources, while on the other lie its various forms of cooperation and the outsourcing that it has carried out. As the figure attempts to express, the more cooperation and outsourcing a company practices, the less resources it needs in order to put its strategy into practice. Or to say the same thing differently, the greater the cooperation and outsourcing, the greater the increase in strategic possibilities for the company given the same resources. This image is as clear as it is important for explaining the current proliferation of cooperation and outsourcing.

10.6 The Corporate Perspective: Integration and Other Diversifications

The last two strategic perspectives we gain from the company value chain are corporate-level visions. This ties in with Chapter 1, in which we

discussed this strategic level, and therefore in this section we will limit ourselves to what is crucial from this perspective for the thinking process we
are engaged in.

From the company value chain perspective, we can analyze whether the
company's strategy would improve, or whether some of its activities would
be performed more optimally, by adding to its current functions an activity
now performed by its supplier or its customer. Therefore, this perspective
helps us to decide about the possibility of carrying out **vertical integration**. For example, the fact that Fiat produces headlights and transmission
systems (which it sells to other car manufacturers) is no more than the addition to the value chain of the Turin company of an activity belonging to its
supplier. We could also mention that the vertical integration of Grifols is
cited by experts in the blood product industry as one of its advantages, as
product procurement and quality are ensured.[5]

Another possible line of thinking from this perspective is the opposite
of outsourcing. The company drops an activity, as we have seen, when it
does not do it very well, or when it is simply not crucial for its strategy.
But the opposite can happen. The company may consider duplicating in
another industry an activity that it performs very well, a function that it
masters, in which it obtains a competitive advantage. This is a **diversification**, because by performing this activity in another industry the company
has a presence in it. For example, large distribution groups such as Carrefour
have travel agencies, taking advantage of the fact that they master the activity of sales. Their basic business provides them with millions of captive
customers with other needs that they can satisfy. Richard Branson's ability to perform the activity of marketing very well since he founded Virgin
in 1970, and so position his brand however he felt was appropriate, is
one of the reasons why the brand has been able to operate in so many
industries.[6]

In Figure 10.9 we add these three last strategic perspectives of
the company value chain (cooperation, vertical integration and other
diversifications) to the GIB model. Thus we can see that there are a total
of six thinking processes to be made from this strategic point of view, having introduced earlier in this chapter the analysis of and decisions about
core activities, strategy in each function, and outsourcing.

We continue to complete the GIB model, conscious of an ever greater
number of strategic perspectives and of the concepts that lie at the root
of this wide range of strategic visions. At the same time we are gaining
greater insight into the interrelationship that exists between each of these
perspectives. We are coming close to having a complete strategic vision,
necessary to be able to make key decisions at business strategy level.

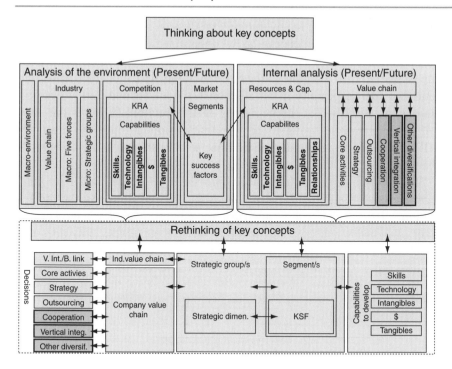

Figure 10.9 Addition to the GIB model of the remaining three strategic perspectives of company value chain analysis

10.7 Relationships

On occasions – obviously to varying degrees depending on the industry concerned – it is not the best value for money that clinches the sale of a product or service or a long-term contract. The essential thing is not necessarily the greatest added value offered. Sometimes the personal relationship between supplier and customer is what really counts.

A personal relationship is cultivated through friendship, membership of the same social or sports club or (deeper still) based on family ties or on having the same beliefs, ways of thinking or ideology. This component of human relationships might not seem to have much to do with the strategic perspectives and concepts described so far, but we cannot neglect to analyze it, as it can be crucial, even decisive, in some industries. This is how lobbies are formed; this is why the representative functions of a general manager or the members of his or her management team are so important.

Therefore, although this is an element that cannot be assimilated to the strategic concepts we have introduced up to now, this perspective should be taken into consideration in any thinking process, as it can be just as strategic as the others, and even decisive, as we mentioned earlier. Indeed, it might show us that certain customers are going to be very difficult (or almost impossible) to deal with due to the close relationship they have with a competitor of ours, especially if this relationship goes beyond purely business reasons, as described at the beginning of this section. If this is the case, it is not worthwhile trying to capture that customer, since the resources will be invested in vain unless their close relationship with our competitor changes.

Hence this vision is introduced into the GIB model in all its main sections: environment and internal analysis and decisions. As we can see in Figure 10.10, relationships appear in the environment as yet another element of industry analysis. At this point we ask ourselves: How does this issue stand in our industry? Are there possible customers who have a close relationship with some competitor based on aspects that are not purely to

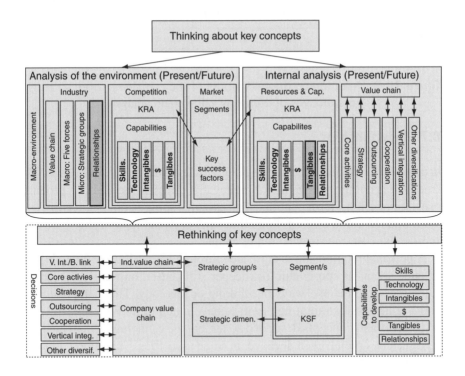

Figure 10.10 Addition of the strategic perspective of relationships to the GIB model

do with business, such as friendship, family ties, beliefs, ways of thinking or ideology?

This analysis of the industry should be complemented with the internal one, specifically the company's capabilities. The organization should think about the relationships it has with its customers. It should think whether it has a strong relationship with any of its customers, based on aspects that are not purely to do with business, such as those described above, and whether it has the necessary capabilities to develop or maintain them.

And these two analyses must converge towards a decision. The company must ask itself, considering the situation of the relationships that exist in its industry and within the firm, whether it should develop some capability in that respect; whether it should take action with a view to building a relationship of interest for its future. This is why decisions about relationships are in the GIB model within the section labeled 'capabilities to develop', as can be seen in Figure 10.10.

The decision might be to develop better a relationship with certain customers, or it might simply be concluded that it is pointless to take any action with some of them until such time as the strong relationship they have with some competitor weakens. Or in some cases we might find that the company's values do not allow it to take the action required from this relationship perspective and so this option is ruled out. We should remember that values underlie any decision.

This last observation should not by any means be taken to mean that relationships should always be assimilated to issues that cast doubt on the ethics or the values of a company. Quite the contrary, it should be taken to mean that whereas many relationships can be entirely ethical and respectful with values, there may be others that do indeed cast doubt on the ethics of the company or some aspect of its values. This latter sort, about which we read more often than we would like in the newspapers, is a matter for the courts to judge.

10.8 Questions for Reflection

I. Taking into account your company's strategy, what are its core activities?[7]

II. What strategy do you seek to achieve in each of the company's activities?

III. At the moment, do you carry out the strategy of each activity better than your competition does?

IV. On the basis of your answers to the questions above, fill in Figure 10.4.

V. Do you fail to achieve your strategy better than your competition does in any of your core activities? If so, might you be able to achieve it in the short run? How? (If you are unable to, you know that you must stop pursuing that strategy, because it is heading for failure.)

Taking into account the result of Figure 10.4:

VI. Should the resources dedicated to one or more of your activities be increased? What activity/activities? What resources?

VII. Could one or more activities be carried out better through some form of internal or external cooperation (strategic alliance, joint venture, merger, acquisition)? What activity/activities? What form of cooperation?

VIII. Could one or more activities be outsourced? What activity/activities? Would outsourcing be appropriate strategically?

IX. Would it be recommendable to carry out vertical integration with the aim of enhancing one or more activities? What sort of vertical integration? What activity/activities would it enhance?

X. Would it be advisable to duplicate in another industry an activity that is performed very well? What activity/activities? In what industry/industries?

XI. Answer the ten questions above again, thinking about the future strategy of your company instead of the present one.

XII. Regarding relationships:

    a. Do they occur in your industry? How important are they?

    b. How do your competitors stand regarding them at the moment? How do you think they will stand in the future?

    c. How does your company stand at the moment? Does it have the capabilities and/or the will to develop or maintain this type of relationship?

    d. Should your company develop capabilities/take action in this respect?

CHAPTER 11

Globalization, Strategy and Internationalization

Sunday 13 September 2009, Sports Cafe, London (80 Haymarket, a stone's throw from Piccadilly Circus), about 6 p.m. After queuing and paying £5, you get access to the two floors of the establishment (where you pay for the drinks at the same price as in any London pub; the entrance fee is for just that, entering). Both floors are packed to the gills. The premises have a licensed capacity for 600 people, and the limits are certainly being put to the test. It's almost impossible to move, and unthinkable to find a decent place. The walls of the pub are lined with huge TV screens. More than 80 percent of the screens are showing Tottenham Hotspur versus Manchester United (1–3), and that proportion of those present focus their eager gaze on that Premier League match. Each goal, especially those of United, is greeted with such a roar that the floor of the building shakes, just as it does whenever there is a missed goal opportunity.

However, there are a few screens that offer alternatives to the match between Spurs and the Red Devils. Hidden away in a corner, two screens are showing Getafe versus FC Barcelona (0-2). Twenty or so people gather round, sacrilegiously turning their backs to the Premier League, to watch how the blue-and-scarlet machine of Messi, Xavi, Iniesta and company start the season. Although they are watching Barcelona, they are perfectly informed of how the Tottenham–United match is going, through the awesome sound system and the roars of the almost 600 souls following that match. At the other end of the same floor, on two other TV screens, a couple of dozen people, whose nationality can be guessed from their appearance, are following Notre Dame versus Michigan (34–38) in the Football NCAA (National Collegiate Athletic Association), the American football college league. Lastly, two more screens, with a few token retinas trained on them, are offering athletics.

Is the Sports Cafe in London an example of the globalization that is taking over a considerable number of industries? Do its owners take advantage of the globalization of the world of sport to respond to it with a global strategy? Those 600 people who filled the place to the brim; were they global customers?

11.1   Global versus Local

It is crucial to analyze the globalization of an industry; the internationalization of its companies depends on it. The globalization of an industry is a fact, a piece of information that is true whether we like it or not, and therefore affects internationalization. A company does not choose the degree of globalization of its industry, but it does choose the degree of its own internationalization, and also the way in which it is carried out. Globalization is – or can be – the cause of internationalization. In other words, according to the degree of globalization of the industry, according to the characteristics of this globalization, the company will be forced to carry out certain internationalization strategies in order to avoid falling into a competitive disadvantage. Nevertheless, it is also true that the company can influence, can try to augment, some of the characteristics of globalization, but only a few.

If an industry is global, the world is *the* industry. Think of the industry of manufacturers of airplanes with more than 100 seats. There are two companies, Boeing and Airbus, competing worldwide in the same way (global competition); consequently the strategy is global, the same the world over. Because their customers, the airlines, are the same the world over. British Airways, Singapore Airlines, Delta, Qantas and South African Airways, although they are based on different continents, have similar needs as far as buying airplanes is concerned. Therefore, the market is also global.

Of course there are distinct segments, as in all markets, since not all customers want exactly the same; some airlines do mainly long-haul flights while others do quite the opposite. Some have both first and business class whereas others only offer economy class, and so on. Airlines' needs differ, but not for geographical reasons. They differ because of the type of need they seek to satisfy, the type of customer they want to attract. Therefore, these segments are the same all over the world; they are global segments. Hence knowledge of the industry is global, as regards both the supply (competition) and the market (customers). As a result, the origin of the resources and the income statement assessment should also be global, to be consistent with the above.

Then, on the other hand, think of a local industry like some foods, or some newspapers. These are industries in which local adaptation comes into its own, as needs are different in each region (country or group of similar countries). In this case, competition is local, on the level of the geographical area delimited by this market, whether this means a continent, a group of countries, one country, or even one area within a country. Therefore, the logical requirement of knowledge of the industry must go hand in hand with in-depth knowledge of the geographical area in which the company is competing. This area is different from others, as its customers have different needs and require local adaptation. Hence the strategy in these cases must be different in each area, and therefore competition too is different in each area. The competitors in each area are different – or perhaps they are the same but carry out a variety of strategies (since they adapt to each area). Consequently, resources usually belong to each area and the income statement is assessed by area, in each market in which the company operates.

As we can see, these are two completely different worlds. We could say that if an industry is 100 percent global it is as if one single world-wide league were played in that industry. All the companies in the industry compete in just one worldwide league. Each company has to train only one team – but it has to be a very good one – and it will compete all over the world. On the other hand, if an industry is 100 percent local it is as if there were as many leagues as local areas exist in that industry (countries, groups of countries, continents or zones). Thus, if a firm wants to compete all over the world it needs to be in each of those leagues. In each one it will train with different teams (diverse strategies) and it will have either different competitors or competitors that, like itself, will adapt to each league with different teams (diverse strategies).

In other words, if a firm is in an industry that is 100 percent global it will perform a single thinking process like the one we have been following with the GIB model. However, if a firm is in a local industry it will have to perform as many thinking processes as areas that industry has. This is only logical, as a different strategy is needed for each of them.

As we said earlier, in local industries we can find companies that operate throughout the world, as obviously occurs by definition in global industries. The sum of local industries forms what we call a multinational industry, a name that points to the fact that originally it was a sum of nations, although nowadays, as we know, it can be made up of a series of geographical areas that may be groups of countries. Therefore, the existence of an industry with companies that operate all over the world is not proof that the industry in question is global. The behavior of the competition will, however, be decisive in this respect. If competition is one and the same all over the world (worldwide strategies), the industry will be global, as everyone will be playing in a single worldwide league. If competition is different in each area (different strategies depending on geographical areas) the industry will be multinational, with different leagues being played in each area.

11.2 Globalization Factors

An industry is seldom either 100 percent global or 0 percent global. Usually an industry has certain global characteristics, to a greater or lesser extent, the rest being local characteristics. As always, the rule is that things are neither black or white but display a range of colors in-between.

In order to know how global an industry is, within it we have to think about the status of a series of factors,[1] each of which, if they are present, favor globalization. These factors also enable us to understand that in recent years there has been a trend toward globalization in most industries. These factors are as follows:

Comparative advantage of countries. Silicon Valley (in the south of San Francisco Bay) has been famous for many years for its high concentration of industries related to semiconductors and computers. This high concentration of high-tech industries favored companies located there due to the high degree of knowledge existing in the area, its high technology and the expertise of its workers. Therefore, if a firm wanted to create value in this type of industry it was attracted to this area, which came to concentrate a high proportion of such companies. Technology parks, science parks and creativity parks (the latest generation of parks) all pursue similar effects. The fact of an area or a country having a competitive advantage (over other countries) favors globalization because it attracts a large number of firms from that industry into the area. These firms are in one place, providing their services throughout the world. Therefore they see the world as a whole, globally.

In the same way, but with the opposite approach, China and Southeast Asia concentrate companies that seek the low costs that the region offers, due above all to the low wages paid in those countries. This also favors globalization, albeit for the opposite reason, because again the region comprises countries with a competitive advantage (costs in this case). Hence the region concentrates many companies from a wide range of industries, which see the world as a single industry, producing for the entire planet from just one part of it.

Global economies of scale. When a particular industry has global economies of scale in one of its activities, enabling this activity to be concentrated in one country, there is a clear trend toward globalization. If R&D can be concentrated in one country, or if it is possible to manufacture at a single plant for the whole world, the planet is being viewed as a single industry in these activities, and so there is a trend toward globalization. The same thing happens with other activities such as logistics, marketing, purchases and so on. The activity of a company that has global economies of scale can be performed for the whole world, with an absolutely global vision, and therefore the industry will tend towards globalization. In marketing, imagine doing a commercial for the whole world, such as Honda's advertisement celebrating the 50th anniversary of its Super Cub in 2008, and the worldwide slogans and commercials for Coca-Cola ("Welcome to the Coke side of life"), Nike ("Just do it"), American Express ("Don't leave home without it"), McDonald's ("I'm loving it") or Apple ("Think different"). The global economies of scale achieved by using a single campaign for the whole planet are no trifle.

Homogenization of customers' needs. When one thinks of globalization, the first companies that come into one's mind are those mentioned above: Coca-Cola, Nike, American Express, McDonald's, Apple or Honda. Why? Primarily because their customers are much the same the world over. Consumers of Coca-Cola, Nike, American Express, McDonald's, Apple and Honda are pretty similar in Shanghai, Indianapolis, Buenos Aires, Sydney and Barcelona. The worldwide homogenization of customers' needs leads to globalization. If customers all over the world demand the same, the company sees the whole planet as a single market, and it will respond to it globally. If Coca-Cola, Nike, American Express, McDonald's, Apple and Honda make global commercials and advertising slogans, all over the world those commercials and slogans match what their customers expect to hear. This is one of the clearest and most easily grasped factors in the globalization of industries. Equally clear is this ever increasing trend towards the homogenization of needs throughout the world.

Although customers may be homogeneous, the fact that the planet is a single market does not mean, as we mentioned earlier, that there are no segments in that global market. If Honda (or Volkswagen group) customers are alike the world over, that it is not to say that there is only one segment in the car market. What it means is that in this market there are segments as in any market, but that they are global segments. In Shanghai, Indianapolis, Buenos Aires, Sydney and Barcelona there are some consumers who want a luxury sports car, others who need a cheap compact family car, and still others who require a small city car. And many more segments we all know, segments that are the same in all those places, indeed all over the world. The size of each segment varies from area to area for several reasons, notably the purchasing power in each region.

Lower transport or storage costs. Imagine an industry with large economies of scale but high transport or storage costs. These costs would cancel out the savings generated by producing in one single place in the world. This is why some goods will never be able to be produced in just one country for the whole world, even if they had global economies of scale. Heavy products (e.g. cement) and/or those that have little added value (e.g. glass bottles) are incompatible with this global vision owing to the high cost involved in transporting them. When we transport glass bottles we are essentially moving air, so factories are located just a few miles from the customers' factories (a totally local vision). The opposite is true of products that weigh little and have a high added value (e.g. watches), which can be easily transported all over the world. The trend toward a lowering of transport and storage costs that has occurred in recent years therefore favors globalization.

Concentration of distribution channels. In the 1960s and 1970s, if a food industry firm located in one country wanted to be present in the rest of the world it had to contact an endless list of distribution companies, each one usually present in one country or a handful of countries, and this hindered the process enormously. Since then the distribution industry has become increasingly concentrated, the number of companies has been reduced significantly, and at the same time their geographical coverage has increased. This process has made it easier for supplier firms to be present throughout the world. Today large companies like Walmart, Carrefour, Tesco, Metro and Aldi (together with Kroger and Target in the USA) concentrate a large part of the industry's sales and are present in many countries. This same phenomenon of concentration of distribution has occurred in other industries, and is another factor that accounts for the trend towards globalization.

Decrease in protectionism. If we think of Europe before the European Community (the precursor of today's European Union), way back in the 1950s, the structure of companies that were present in several countries was above all national, the country perspective being predominant. For example, Philips was organized into Philips Netherlands, Philips France, Philips Spain and so on; each country was a separate market, as its borders constituted a major – sometimes insurmountable – barrier to the entry of outside products or services. Nowadays this national vision is unthinkable as the principal structure of the company (although subsidiaries continue to exist at national level). Thus, Philips today is organized into divisions: health-care, lighting, consumer products and lifestyle.

Protectionism is an artificial barrier to globalization. It builds political walls that block this vision of the world as a single market. There has been a clear worldwide decrease in protectionism in recent years. Europe provided a spectacular example of the removal of these artificial barriers with the creation of the European Union. The EU, after successive enlargements since its foundation in 1957 (with six member states), as of 2007 comprised 27 states amounting to a market of some 500 million people. This trend toward the disappearance of protectionism at world level, with some steps backwards, logically favors globalization.

Global experience curve. As we discussed in Chapter 3, if learning is accumulated by performing an activity there will be a decrease in costs and/or the activity will be performed better, as know-how will be optimized. The activity is done better and/or at a lower cost as experience accumulates. This learning process can also take place on a global scale if this progress occurs anywhere in the world that the activity is performed, if it is similar regardless of the geographical area. If it is not global, experience in one geographical area will be different from experience in another, and cannot be accumulated. For example, if the markets of different countries or regions have different needs, experience cannot be accumulated on a global scale in the areas of marketing and sales, whereas it can if the markets are global.

Technological development. Technological development undeniably helps us to see the world as a single unit, and therefore favors globalization. Telecommunications make it possible to work, even in real time, with people who live thousands of miles away as if they were in the next office. They enable the world population to connect to each other, doing away with the sensation of distance. Global media (television, press, radio) are a force for the homogenization of the population of the planet, making for matching tastes and converging needs. Security of means of payment in all types of transactions allows us to make purchases on the other side of the world without even leaving our office or home. Without the technological development that has occurred in recent years, the trend towards globalization would have been much slower.

By thinking about all these factors we can conclude about the degree of globalization in an industry. As an additional help in this thinking process, these factors can be simplified by placing them in four main groups:[2]

- **Demand factors:** The homogenization of customers' needs, the standardization of the market, the existence of the same segments all over the world, account for globalization from the demand side, from the market. Companies can target the world as a single market if it is global.

- **Supply factors:** The increase in global economies of scale, the global experience curve, the comparative advantage of countries, account for globalization from a supply perspective, in terms of the supply obtaining lower costs or greater value. Companies perform better or at a lower cost if they take advantage of this global vision from the supply side, from what they do.

- **Technological factors:** Technological development, digitalization, telecommunications and so on make possible, facilitate enormously, a unitary way of thinking about our planet, wherever we may be. This minimizes distances and homogenizes nations, races and cultures, no matter how different they are.

- **Political factors:** The destruction of political barriers, the eradication of protectionism, liberalization, deregulation, allow globalization in the world, by removing one of the most important artificial obstacles.

With this information a company can conclude which globalization factors are present in its industry and consequently how globalized it is. In itself, this information does not seem very relevant, but it is a stepping stone to other information that is entirely relevant, as it will enable the company to decide how to go about its internationalization process.

11.3 Globalization and Company Activities

If we merge the globalization perspective that we have just described, the factors that lead an industry toward this unitary vision of the world, with the company value chain perspective described in Chapter 10, we can draw some interesting conclusions.

As we have already mentioned, it is unusual to find either all the globalization factors (when an industry is 100 percent global) or none of them (when it is 100 percent local). Usually an industry has one or more of the factors analyzed.

If an industry is totally global, all the activities of its companies are global. Conversely, if an industry is totally local (0 percent global), none of its activities is global. And if an industry is partially global, that is, if it displays only certain globalization factors, only certain activities will be global.

For example, if in a given industry we find only demand factors, its customers being similar and the market segments being the same the world over, the company can carry out the activity of marketing globally. This is when, for example, companies can consider having global slogans or commercials, as in the cases of Coca-Cola, Nike, American Express, McDonald's, Apple and Honda described at the beginning of this chapter.

On the other hand, if the globalization factors that are present in an industry are supply factors, if for example there are global economies of scale, comparative advantage of countries and/or global experience curve in operations, it is this activity that will be global. Companies in such industries usually manufacture in one country for the whole world in order to take advantage of economies of scale, experience and/or the competitive advantage of countries (as long as transport costs and time allow, of course). Logically, if global economies of scale occur in R&D activity, this will be the global area.

In short, if an industry is neither 100 percent or 0 percent global, only some of its activities will be global. This is an essential conclusion for the strategy of a company, because if a particular activity is global the company must either perform it globally or bear a competitive disadvantage relative to its competitors who do perform it globally. If marketing is global because customers are homogeneous all over the world, and our company only operates in one continent, we will be at a disadvantage vis-à-vis global brands. The latter will take greater advantage of their global knowledge and image, and also the global economies of scale that exist in marketing. The same thing will happen with any activity that is global but is approached on a more local level.

This is not to say that there cannot be degrees of globalization in an activity. The well-known phrase "think globally, act locally" conveys this idea. Even the most global brands, those that do the most global marketing, have some degree of local adaptation. Coca-Cola does not have the same product portfolio in all its markets; it knows that formats and tastes have a certain local component that is worth respecting in each country. Similarly, the form of distribution may differ according to the country. Things are hardly ever black and white; the totalitarian vision of the world has fewer and fewer supporters.

Thus, having thought about globalization factors and company activities, we can ask ourselves whether the industries in which Coca-Cola, Nike, American Express, McDonald's, Apple and Honda operate are absolutely global, or whether they are so only in some factors, and therefore only in some activities. In fact, only the industry of American Express could be considered practically 100 percent global, and therefore with almost entirely global activities, although Apple's would be close, and it would be Coca-Cola's if we think just in the concentrate producers and not in the bottling business.

11.4 Globalization and Market Segments

When the demand factors mentioned above are fully present, customers are similar all over the world and therefore all market segments are global. However, we may find that even when the market is not global, when all customers are not homogeneous everywhere on the planet, one or more market segments may nevertheless be global.

If we take the luxury segment, we find that it is global in almost all markets, even when the rest of those respective markets are not. In markets such as watches, handbags and accessories, clothes, jewelry, hotels, drinks and so on, luxury is global whereas the rest of the market is less so. For example, demand for the luxury segment in hotels is homogeneous worldwide; customers of luxury hotels demand exactly the same whether they are in Singapore, Madrid, New York, Melbourne, Tokyo or Johannesburg. Therefore companies in this segment follow the same strategy all over the world. The brand – brand recognition and image in this segment – is an important dimension of their strategy, because as their customers travel far and wide, they tend to be loyal to brands that identify with the satisfaction of luxury as those individuals understand and need it. Hence the firms who operate in this segment compete globally. The chains Starwood (Sheraton, Westin, Le Meridien), Hilton (Waldorf Astoria, Conrad, Hilton), Hyatt, Intercontinental and Sofitel hotels (belonging to Accor) compete in a world league of the segment of luxury hotels.

Furthermore, the various luxury segments may not be the only global ones. If we think of the audiovisual market, to be more exact TV channels, we find that here too there is a global segment, targeted by the CNN network, for example. Likewise, there is a national segment, covered by the various channels that broadcast at that level, for example NBC, ABC and CBS in the United States. At the same time there are other segments within a smaller geographical area; for instance in the United States we find WTHR Channel 13 in Indianapolis and WTIU TV 30 in Bloomington, also in Indiana. There are even neighborhood channels, for example Manhattan Neighborhood Network, in this neighborhood of New York. So, as we can see, there is everything from a global segment to absolutely local ones, including a wide range of intermediate segments.

Combining the comments we have made about global segments, companies and media, we could mention the commercial aired by the hotel chain InterContinental on CNN a few years ago, which said simply: "One world, one hotel". A global commercial for a global company on global media.

It should also be taken into consideration that a product may be global as regards demand, the market, inasmuch as it is sold worldwide, yet be in different segments depending on the geographical area concerned. Corona is a world-famous Mexican beer in the Modelo group.[3] However, whereas in many countries it is regarded as a high-quality, high-price beer, in Mexico it was developed as the beer of the workers, a lower price segment.

This is a possibility that is worth thinking about: a brand (a product or service) can be positioned in different segments in different geographical areas of the world, according to the characteristics of that area, its purchasing power and so on. And at all times we must bear in mind the total and absolute dynamism of all aspects of company strategy. As a result, if this different positioning depending on geographical areas occurs, it will evolve over time, like all the other strategic concepts that comprise the GIB model.

11.5 Almost Closing the Circle of Globalization

To sum up, we can distinguish three stages in strategic thinking about the globalization of an industry:

■ Globalization factors occurring in an industry

And, as a consequence of this first analysis, we can conclude:

■ Activities in the company value chain that are global

■ Market segments that are global

If at this point we go back to our initial example of the Sports Cafe in London, we are now in a position to answer the questions we had left hanging in the air. On 13 September 2009, this London mega-pub was packed with three market segments: Premier League viewers watching Tottenham

Hotspur play Manchester United – the vast majority – and two minorities following the Spanish league match (Getafe versus Barcelona) and the American football university league game (Notre Dame versus Michigan). Were they global segments? Considering that the immense majority of the Premier League spectators were British, those watching the Spanish league were Spanish, and those watching the American football university league were American, the answer is no. They were local segments, some of them watching their match thousands of miles from home. It was the technology that was global, the technology that allowed the Sports Cafe in London to satisfy these very different needs felt by people from distant places.

Another issue is the growing globalization of sport. This forms an important part of the business model and the strategy being developed by the most powerful clubs. Why are the pre-seasons of FC Barcelona, Real Madrid and Manchester United played in America or Asia, with the fatigue this involves for their team members? Why did Real Madrid pay almost €100 million for Cristiano Ronaldo? Why was the final of the FIFA Club World Cup played in Japan (2008), Abu Dhabi (2009) and the United Arab Emirates (2010), all countries without any possibility of winning it? Why was the final of the 2009 Italian Supercup between Lazio and Inter (2–1) played in Beijing? Why is the Spanish league studying the possibility of scheduling matches at 3 p.m. (TV prime time in China)? There is one single answer to all these questions: because the aim is to globalize sport, in this case soccer, by attracting spectators all over the world, by trying to get clubs to have supporters all over the world. When this is achieved, when the Sports Cafe in London is packed with people from all over the world, all as one watching a Real Madrid versus Barcelona match, an NFL or NCAA American football game, or an NBA one, then its customers will be global. Those of September 2009 were not; each was following the championship of his or her own country.

This does not mean that there is not already a considerable global segment in all these sports. Nowadays viewers in countries throughout the world watch NBA, NFL and Champions League matches. The author of this book saw the 2009 final of this last competition between Barcelona and Manchester United (2–0) in Montevideo, and he was not alone. A global segment already exists; there are already people all over the world following, on a weekly basis, teams based thousands of miles away. The 2010 soccer World Cup final between Spain and the Netherlands (1–0) was watched by more than 700 million people worldwide. This is the reason for the existence of global strategies such as those of the powerful European football teams, for example.

If we introduce the globalization factor into the GIB model, this will change our perspective of the environment, as we have seen and is shown in

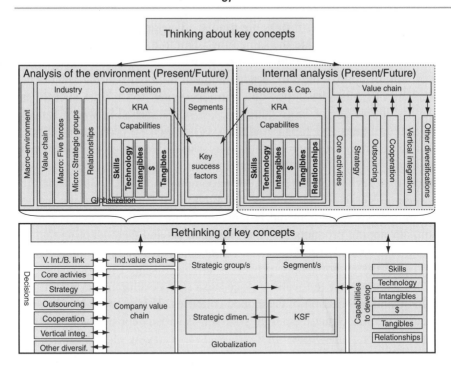

Figure 11.1   Addition of globalization to the GIB model

Figure 11.1. It is no longer a question of thinking about all the components of the macro environment, industry, competition or market of one geographical area, but on a worldwide scale, at least in those parts of the environment that are global.

Figure 11.1 also highlights that globalization affects the decisions of the company, the segments it targets, its decisions about the value chain or capabilities; even the business model, the mission, are influenced by the degree of globalization in the industry. The company must make decisions on the basis of the degree of globalization of its industry.

11.6   Glocalization and Reverse Innovation

Glocalization is the process employed by many large First World companies over the last three decades to develop their high-performance products, designed for their markets, and subsequently adapt them to local conditions in developing or underdeveloped countries, which usually meant simplifying features and lowering prices. This process was carried out for many years, as it made it possible to take advantage of the various global economies of scale and at the same time adapt to the local market.

However, as of the end of 2009, glocalization has ceased to be the only way of approaching local adaptation in a global world.[4] It had been until then because developed countries accounted for a large slice of the worldwide market for large companies. It was a period in which Europe, the United States and Japan could amass between 80 percent and 90 percent (sometimes even more) of many markets. But the great development attained by highly populated countries like China and India, together with others that have undergone rapid development, such as Canada, Australia, Brazil and Russia, in addition to the Middle East, has changed the picture. For Immelt, Govindarajan and Trimble the future also lies in reverse innovation, developing products for emerging markets and then adapting them to the more advanced economies, that is, the opposite process to glocalization.

For these authors, both processes are necessary. Big companies are forced to do reverse innovation, since success in developing economies is a prerequisite for triumph in developed countries. This is so for two reasons: because the size of these emerging markets is already considerable, and also to prevent companies based in those countries carrying out the reverse process and ultimately penetrating the advanced countries, thus becoming new giants.

The two models should not only coexist but also cooperate, although obviously whereas glocalization works from the basis of centralization in the initial development of the global product, reverse innovation requires decentralization, as its point of origin is the needs of local markets. In fact, reverse innovation is initially a local industry conception that finally takes on a global industry perspective. This is just the opposite of glocalization, which starts from a global initial conception and ends up with a totally local viewpoint.

Another factor that differs between these two processes and conceptions is which activities are global and should be performed as such. This is derived from the different time process they follow with regard to the global conception, as we have just seen. In the early stages of glocalization most activities tend to be global, subsequently becoming local. This global beginning and local end affects R&D and marketing in particular, since in other activities, notably operations, it will depend on the extent to which they display global economies of scale and the various other globalization factors described above.

In reverse innovation we find the opposite: the initial conception is essentially local for all activities, again in R&D and marketing particularly. Advantage is taken of the company's knowledge, of course, but with a local vision and organization. Later, when this local vision and organization have proved successful, it is transferred to a global vision, and activities can become global (especially R&D and marketing). If both conceptions exist side by side as we have mentioned, both ways of performing activities, and therefore different organizations, will also have to coexist.

We can also think about these two conceptions from the perspective of market segments. In the case of glocalization, the global upper segment, that represented by the United States, the European Union and Japan, was far superior to the more local lower segment, practically "the rest of the world", which allowed this vision to predominate. In the case of reverse innovation, the more local (multinational) lower segment has grown enough to be taken into account and for an initial strategy to be developed from it.

Given that the trend is for the two segments (global and local, i.e. multinational) to coexist in more and more industries, the need arises for both processes (glocalization and reverse innovation) to be carried out simultaneously. Therefore, some activities of the company will be at the same time global in one case (glocalization) and local in the other (reverse innovation), which means that the company must have two different strategies and so a different organization to deal with each strategy.

11.7 Internationalization

As we have seen, analyzing the globalization of the industry entails making decisions about internationalization, about performing one or more activities outside the country of origin. At one extreme, if the industry is global, if all the globalization factors are present, if all the company's activities are global, if the market is global, the company should carry out a single strategy, considering the world as a single industry or market. Thus its various activities can be concentrated in one country, possibly with different countries for each activity: R&D could be in one country, manufacturing in another, and so on. The company will be forced to carry out an in-depth internationalization process, at the risk of being at a competitive disadvantage to the rest of the companies in the industry if it does not do so.

On the other hand, if the industry is not at all global, if it is local, the internationalization process will not be so obligatory. If the company operates in just one country or a set of countries (those that make up the local market) it will not have the competitive disadvantage we saw in the case of the global industry. The internationalization process can be carried out in a much more relaxed fashion, or it can even be abandoned. The company could study what new leagues (geographical areas) to enter, to use the metaphor employed earlier to distinguish local industries from global ones.

Whether an industry is global or not, internationalization is no more than one of the options available to a company in order to grow, and as such may be a very interesting option even if it is not imposed by globalization. As far back as 20 years ago it was concluded that the reasons for which Spanish companies decided to internationalize had ceased to be purely defensive, reactive, and had become a central element of company strategy.[5]

There are several possible defensive reasons to internationalize. The company's product might be in the maturity phase (low growth rate) in the national market, so the only option for growth might be foreign markets. Or the company's customers might internationalize and force it to follow them. Alternatively, a part of the company's production capacity might be idle, and so the company might try to find an outlet for it through export. Another reason can be that foreign competitors might enter the country, causing the company to react and try to find a space in their markets. On the other hand, examples of proactive reasons would be to achieve larger economies of scale (possible in several value chain activities), to develop better technology or know-how, or to adapt the company's products or services to foreign markets.

11.8 Risks of Internationalization

If a firm moves on from operating in just one country to doing so internationally, it may have to take a series of risks in addition to those it already had. These risks may or may not be relevant, depending on the region of the planet that is being penetrated and the form of internationalization that is chosen.

Financial risks. If the countries in which the company is going to operate have a currency other than that of the country of origin, fluctuations in the exchange rate may result in its competitiveness and profits being greatly affected, sometimes favorably, sometimes negatively. And the effect is always the opposite for companies that import from or export to the country concerned. As an example of how the value of currencies can change, we could cite the case of the euro against the dollar. The euro first went onto the market in January 1999, at $1.17. However, by October 2000 the single European currency had fallen to $0.82, a 35 percent depreciation in less than two years. Yet in July 2008 it reached $1.60, an appreciation of almost 100 percent over October 2000! These fluctuations occur with all currencies; between 2000 and 2002 a euro was worth between £0.57 and £0.65 sterling, whereas during 2009 the two currencies almost reached parity, with a devaluation of the British currency in excess of 50 percent. It is true that an organization can hedge its currency exposure, but such insurance policies have a fluctuation limit linked to the value at the time of underwriting, as well as representing an additional cost.

Another risk of this type is the different inflation rate that may occur in different countries. This unequal inflation will make the companies of each country more competitive or less so, by raising to a lesser or greater extent their labor, financial or raw material costs.

Political risks. "Nationalize it! There's nothing to discuss!" said the Venezuelan president, Hugo Chávez, in May 2009,[6] as he ordered the expropriation of the iron briquette (metallurgical) industry, a total of six companies in the mining region of Guayana, in the state of Bolívar. Two of them belonged to the Argentinean group Techint. "These companies should be under worker control," he added. That month he had already expropriated 10,000 hectares with the aim of providing backing for policies to break up large estates with fallow land and encourage food production. Earlier, in March the same year, he had announced, within the framework of his socialist "agrarian revolution", the seizure of 1500 hectares of land belonging to the Venezuelan subsidiary of the Irish multinational Smurfit Kappa Group, which makes paper. Previous to that, he had expropriated companies such as Cargill for "violating" local laws that guarantee the population access to cheap quality food, together with 70 oil service companies in the west of the country. The list would be extremely long, as the process of Hugo Chávez's expropriations has extended over years, affecting innumerable industries. In August 2009, after taking temporary control of two coffee companies, Chávez announced that he would carry on with the nationalizations, as he would, in his own words, "continue to step on the gas of the revolution".[7]

In 2010 he did so with even greater intensity with all sorts of goods. For example, in February he ordered, with the remark "Expropriate it, Mayor," the confiscation of a number of buildings around the capital's Plaza Bolívar. He then went on to expropriate the hypermarket chain Éxito, controlled by the French group Casino. One of his priorities continued to be control over the media, as was shown by his attempt to control the television channel Globovisión, in open opposition to his regime. From 2005 to 2010, the expropriations amounted to over a thousand. The feeling of insecurity of any company considering Hugo Chávez's country as a destination for its investments is obvious.

Iran under Ahmadinejad and North Korea under Kim Jong-Il have provided similar examples of what "political risk" means for a company (together with a very high physical risk for their internal opponents). Less brutal examples are the reprisals taken in some industries between the European Union and the United States. We could also mention here the case of a firm that does business with both Israel and Arab countries: the firm might lose some of its customers if it comes to their attention that the firm also has dealings with their neighbors.

Legislative and regulatory risks. Technical standards or official approval are intended to protect consumers in each country as regards the health, quality or safety standards of imported products. But they have often been used as protectionist measures, to force exporters to meet these standards, simply in order to cause them an additional cost or prevent them from entering the country. Also, sometimes they derive from political decisions, and as such can be instruments of the risk discussed above. One of the consequences of the EU has been the harmonization to a large extent of the respective legislations in the member countries.

Tax risks. Depending on the country, there may be (to a greater or lesser extent and importance) capital transfer taxes, tariffs, restrictions on repatriation of profits, variations in the size of corporate tax, and so on.

Institutional differences. In a new country the company has to start from scratch with regard to knowledge of the workings of government bodies, capital markets or trade unions. This factor will be more important or less so, depending on the type of country concerned.

Cultural differences. Furthermore, depending on the country in question, there may be cultural differences because of the gap between languages, tastes, customs and so on. This may occur between staff from the parent company and local staff, and also in the approach to the new market. One example of this lack of understanding of local customs is the experience of a certain manufacturer of slimming products. The company set up in an Arab country, where people read from right to left. When they inserted an advertisement for their product in the local press they had all the copy translated, but they failed to realize that they also needed to reverse the position of the "before" and "after" photos. Naturally, their initial sales were practically zero.

If these institutional, cultural, legislative and other differences are very large, in most cases it is highly recommendable to have a native bridgehead, in the form of either an individual or a partner firm. This will help the company to have a smoother time discovering the new culture and the different way of doing things.

11.9   Stages of Internationalization

Years ago, internationalization was described as a gradual process that occurs in stages,[8] although entry to the international market can be gained by means of any of these stages, thus skipping some of them.[9] These stages can be summarized as follows:[10]

Occasional exports. Merely reactive; the company responds to sporadic orders received from abroad.

Experimental exports. It is the company that decides to start the internationalization process, which is therefore a proactive decision. Usually it is a case of exporting surplus production and using intermediaries (agents or export companies).

Regular exports. Part of the production is earmarked for export. The company has stable customers abroad, and usually an export department.

Establishing subsidiaries abroad. Human and financial resources are invested abroad (such as warehouse, inventories, offices, marketing campaigns).

Establishing production subsidiaries abroad. This is virtually the final stage (as the process is seldom extended to R&D). The value chain has almost been duplicated abroad.

At each stage the company has increased its obligations in regard to resources, and therefore also its risk, in return increasing the extent of its control and its potential profit.

Other forms of evolution have been described in which internationalization goes hand in hand with diversification. For example, Vives and Mendoza describe how Abengoa went through an initial cash generation stage in those activities that the company mastered.[11] This first stage led to a second stage marked by growth, both of lines of business and of geographical presence. Finally there was a third stage involving future options. As a result of this process Abengoa went from depending on engineering to being a diversified group with four main business areas and very substantial geographical expansion.

As we have already mentioned, whether a firm chooses one internationalization strategy or another, and how rapidly it does so, will be influenced above all by the degree of globalization that exists in the industry, that is, which activities and/or segments are global. It will also depend on other external factors, and some internal ones. Among the external factors, apart from the appeal of the market, we can cite the following:[12] macro-economic conditions, political environment, infrastructures, similarity of cultural norms and social structures, and magnitude of the risks (as described above). Among the internal factors, the following should be taken into consideration: characteristics of the technology and the products, availability of production capacity in the country of origin, minimum volume of a new plant, availability of financial and human resources, and level of risk the company is prepared to take. Often one of the main difficulties is the availability of suitable staff. Companies are usually quite short on people who are good all-rounders. Sometimes in order to facilitate the internationalization process it is recommendable to set up some sort of alliance or joint venture with other companies.

With the addition of the perspectives of globalization and internationalization we have completed the formation of the GIB model, as shown in Figure 11.2.

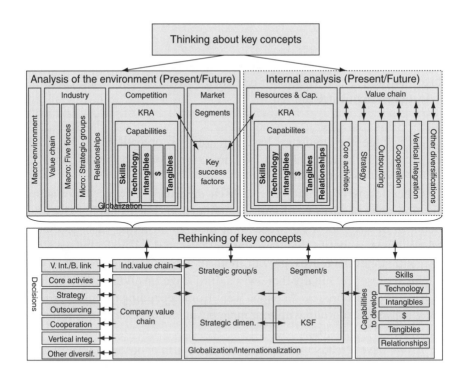

Figure 11.2 The GIB model

11.10 Questions for Reflection

I. What degree of globalization is there in your industry? What globalization factors does it possess?

II. Considering the above, are some of its activities global? Which?

III. If your market is not global, are there global segments?

IV. Does glocalization occur in your industry?

V. Does reverse innovation occur in your industry?

VI. Does your company's strategy take the above questions into account?

VII. If instead of thinking about the present situation you ask yourself the above questions thinking about the medium and long term (however long you consider reasonable for this type of thinking in your industry), what will your answers be?

VIII. If your answers to the first five questions are now different, what changes should you make to your strategy in the future?

IX. Considering your answers to the above questions, is your internationalization strategy the right one?

X. What stage or stages of the internationalization process is your company in at the moment?

XI. What risks of internationalization has your company had to take?

XII. What changes will you make to your internationalization strategy in the future?

CHAPTER 12

Strategy and Crisis

In mid-July 2007, the collapse of two Bear Stearns hedge funds triggered a crisis that will make history for its extraordinary global virulence. Its most devastating effects, the virtual breakdown of the system, planetary terror, were not to be felt until 2008, but then lasted (albeit with less fear of systemic apocalypse) right through 2009 and 2010, while in 2011 its aftermath is still affecting some countries, mainly among the developed world. We should recall that this crisis was first a financial one, with huge losses for many institutions in that industry and their customers. Losses were so great that they cast doubt on the whole system; the world shook when a giant such as Lehman Brothers fell. Only the historic intervention by all the main central banks stopped panic developing into the most profound chaos.

This crisis, extremely harmful to the financial sector, spread to the real economy, causing not only heavy losses but also an almost total evaporation of liquidity. Money disappeared, and with it banks' ability to lend money to companies. Lack of funding caused many businesses to go under at a time when, domino-like, industry after industry caught the crisis in the same way as swine flu spread worldwide around that time. Sales plummeted in one industry after another, in some cases by more than 50 percent. Massive layoffs only served to aggravate the crisis still further in most industries. In the face of this radical economic change, customers varied their demands and needs, becoming much more fickle and demanding, and watching every cent they spent. Even customers who still wielded purchasing power felt psychologically affected by the environment, behaving with the same exigency and variability as those around them.

The brutal drop in sales, the much more demanding habits of customers and the much weaker (sometimes almost non-existent) borrowing capacity of companies raised competition to previously unseen levels in almost all industries.

12.1 Effects of A Crisis on Strategic Management

As we have seen in the course of our development of the GIB model, strategic management is no more than the process of constant adaptation by the company to its environment in an attempt to always be better than its competitors in some vital aspect that is valued by its customers, or at least for the minimum number of customers to ensure its survival. How does a crisis affect this process? In two main ways. First, if the business environment is usually turbulent and influenced by a host of variables that change both rapidly and unpredictably, in times of crisis this turbulence is magnified; change is even more rapid and unpredictable. Second, change is usually for the worse; the tendency is for the situation to deteriorate, in the economy, the industry and the market alike. It is also true that opportunities can arise, but they are always harder to come by than threats. Thus there are two terrible effects for the company: even more turbulence, which makes forecasting less effective, and a tendency for the situation to deteriorate.

This amounts to a great added difficulty when it comes to strategy. However, despite this difficulty, and for the same reasons that cause it, in times of crisis the company has an almost inescapable need to reconsider its strategy. If everything changes, and changes very rapidly and for the worse, clearly no one can stand still. To do so would be tantamount to giving up on the future. Moreover, we can say that this need for strategic change is virtually constant for the same reasons; the turbulence of the environment demands persistent attention to it.

In short, strategy becomes a permanent thinking exercise, under penalty of the company falling by the wayside without even knowing it, as was the case of so many organizations between 2007 and 2011. Figure 12.1 sums up these effects of a crisis on strategic management.

However, a crisis such as the one that occurred between 2007 and 2011 can also have a positive strategic reading. If we succeed in making strategy into a permanent thinking exercise we will improve our organization not just to get through the crisis but to face the future, no matter what it holds in store. Furthermore, in the words of Clayton Christensen, "The breakthrough innovations come when the tension is greatest and the resources are most limited. That's when people are actually a lot more open to rethinking the fundamental way they do business." [1] And what time has greater tension and more limited resources than a crisis?

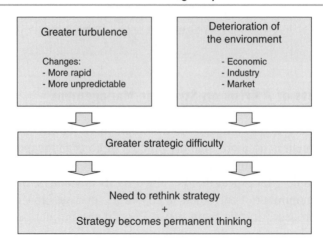

Figure 12.1 Effects of a crisis on strategic management

Other authors have generalized this idea, seeing crises as a great opportunity – as long as one reacts, as long as one thinks strategically, as long as one has a point of view that is consistent with the competitive situation.[2] In short, as long as one thinks about broad future trends. To quote Vijay Govindarajan, "There's a big difference between planning for the future and preparing for it. Preparing for the future simply involves asking what the broad trends are."[3]

Another positive effect of a conflictive period such as a crisis is that talent, the key strategic characteristic, together with other essential assets, are easier to find and less expensive to acquire. Figure 12.2 summarizes these positive effects of a crisis on company strategy; therefore, it does not mention the positive effects it might also have on other important areas of the company such as its structure or its organizational culture.

At the beginning of 2009 the consultancy firm Arthur D. Little conducted a study based on a survey of more than 360 top managers in major industries all over the world.[4] The analysis highlighted that nine out of ten managers interviewed saw the crisis as an opportunity to differentiate themselves and consolidate their markets. They considered that the crisis could have a cleansing effect in their industries, by getting rid of the weakest competitors. The conclusion drawn was that businesses that emerge in periods of crisis have more agile business models and can benefit from better costs through economies of scale. According to the results of the study, the uncertainty generated by the global crisis had caused 73 percent of those

Figure 12.2 Positive effects of a crisis on strategic management

Source: Based on Mangelsdorf, C., Rumelt, R. and Govindarajan, V.

interviewed to rethink their way of doing business and question the sustainability of traditional models, undoubtedly positive effects of the financial and economic crisis.

The positive strategic effects of this devastating crisis were also reaffirmed by another study made public in June 2009 by the consultancy firm KPMG after having interviewed 852 senior businesspeople with responsibility over decision-making in their respective organisations.[5] These companies, based in 29 countries, were from all sectors of the economy and had annual revenue ranging from $250 million to $5000 million. Although its title, "Never catch a falling knife" (a literal quote from one of the respondents), summed up perfectly the uncertainty felt by many companies across the globe in the face of the crisis and its consequences, its conclusions again pointed to the clear strategic awakening it produced. A large proportion of companies, especially in Asia (Japan being at the head, with 90 percent of its companies), claimed to have used the global recession as an opportunity to make substantial changes in their business strategy as a way of reacting to the new environment.

Either way, whether we focus on the negative or the positive side of a crisis, one thing is clear: the more turbulent the business environment is, the fewer safe things we have to hang on to, the faster the changes are, the larger the global crisis is – the more the company needs strategic management. Strategic management understood as taking on board a handful of unrenounceable key concepts which we have to be absolutely clear about, yet at the same have to be constantly re-examined, as they change both rapidly and unpredictably.

And this is the key point of strategy in times of crisis. The company must rethink what it does. Strategy has to be a constant thinking process.

But we cannot think continuously about many concepts, as we run the risk of becoming distracted, when it is vital to avoid this, as we have already mentioned. The more complex the environment, the more simply the strategy should be defined; the hazier the surroundings, the clearer we need to be about the competitive advantage. This does not guarantee the survival of the company but it does help it to stay in with a fighting chance, as long as a constant effort is made to respond to the ongoing changes posed by customers, competitors and the economic situation.

In short, in order to face the greater complexity, the constant changes and the deterioration associated with a crisis, it is recommendable to have a very clear and synthetic view of strategy, of the key pieces of the strategy of the company. Only from a clear and synthetic perspective of strategy, of its essential constituent parts, can we face this complexity and make decisions in real time, as changes in key aspects of the environment occur.

12.2 Some Strategic Guidelines for Management in Times of Crisis or Turbulent Periods

In Chapter 1 we presented two opposing ways of thinking and deciding about strategy: planned strategy and emergent strategy (these are the two extremes, but there are also middle ways). In the case of planned strategy, the strategy was decided by means of a rational, formalized and systematic process. Analyses were performed stage by stage, then several alternatives were evaluated, and finally a decision was made. All this was done over a relatively long period of time. In contrast, in the second option the strategy emerged out of a more incremental, accumulative and intuitive process of thinking and decision-making. This type of process was almost instantaneous, as strategy arose as a response to rapid and unexpected changes in the environment.

Logically, in times of crisis (or turbulent periods) a highly planned decision-making process is no good to us. There is no time. Changes in the environment (economy, market and industry) are so fast and unpredictable that a company cannot afford to think for very long. In the midst of a crisis (or at moments of great complexity) the process of strategic decision-making will tend to be emergent. We will have to adapt to a highly changing and unforeseeable reality in real time, almost instantly.

And although it might seem to suggest the opposite, this highlights even more the need for strategic models like the GIB model developed in the preceding chapters (or the strategic core model, which we will develop in the next chapter). Knowing and understanding the key strategic concepts that affect the company and its interrelationships is the best way to foster instant thinking and snap decision-making in the face of the volatility of the environment.

In the case of emergent strategies, these models serve as mindsets rather than as guides to a highly detailed thinking process. That is, we should use them as knowledge support in this almost instantaneous thinking and decision-making process. Thanks to them, we know what concepts are key and how they are interrelated. In this way we can interpret more rapidly what the unexpected change in the environment means for our business and we will come to a decision with more agility. In other words, the mindset helps us to see through the great complexity of the environment and rapidly identify the key variables and the essential aspect about which we must reach a decision.

So, in times of crisis or periods of great turbulence, senior managers cannot seek a safe haven in highly planned processes of strategic formulation. However, they must be confident that their managers are well acquainted with the planning models and have experience in this type of thinking.

In fact, in tricky competitive situations it is not always senior management who hits on future strategic solutions. Sometimes the brilliant ideas and the answers to the chaos can come from people who work lower down the ladder. They might come, for example, from people who know the market, the customers, very well – people who are in close everyday contact with them, know their needs, notice changes in them, sense new trends.

To summarize, the managing director or CEO of a firm is ultimately responsible for strategy, and naturally must be fully involved in the leadership of the strategic process. Nevertheless, in critical situations – and also in not so serious ones – it is wise to open up the spectrum of thinking and accept proposals from the maximum possible number of workers. It is essential to motivate the organization about the importance of its contribution. It may even be advisable to create thinking groups by areas or departments so that they can collaborate in the process. It is a good thing to be humble and flexible and listen carefully to any strategic proposal, no matter where it comes from.

In times of crisis or complexity it is more important than ever to be aware of the value of people. After all, it is they who will mark the future of the company. It is people who analyze and decide on strategy. A united management team that draws together the whole organization, that gets information and knowledge flowing through all the layers and areas of the company, everyone learning from everyone else, working with passion and passing these qualities on to all their fellow workers, is almost unbeatable.

Innovation should be ingrained in the culture, in the values of the company and in the consciousness of each employee. Increasingly, competitive advantage depends on creativity. In order for innovation to be truly ingrained in company culture, a climate must be created that allows error and the learning that comes as a result. A competitive advantage is not created with the first idea, but after many.

In times of crisis or periods of great complexity, everything that matters is in short supply, and that includes time. But it would be a mistake to find stopgap solutions for today without taking tomorrow into account. Time must be dedicated to thinking strategically. We should not worry if this consumes part of this extremely scarce good. It's the old story about whether to eat fish today or learn how to fish. The answer is clear.

To sum up, difficult does not mean impossible, by any means. As we said in the introduction, strategic management is change; it has the immense and wonderful power to transform, to innovate, to create. As long ago as the mid-1990s,[6] Richard Branson, creator and owner of Virgin, said: "People think politicians can change the world, but it's not true. The only people who have real power are us businesspeople."[7] This is the strength of strategic management.

12.3 Questions for Reflection

    I. What were the main effects of the crisis of 2007–2011 on your industry?

    II. What did your company learn from that crisis?

    III. What strategic changes did it make?

    IV. Is your company ready to detect the next crisis before it strikes?

    V. Are the senior managers of your company properly acquainted with all the key variables of its strategy and how they are interrelated?

    VI. Is the staff of your organization given the chance to make suggestions about the company's business or functional strategy? Is this collaboration encouraged?

    VII. Do information and knowledge flow through the various areas of your organization?

    VIII. Are innovation and creativity valued and encouraged in your company? Is error allowed, as a means to nurture creativity and achieve innovations, valuing the learning that comes as a result?

CHAPTER 13

The Strategic Core Model

The world will never go back to the way it was before 2007. In the wake of the 2007–2011 crisis nothing will ever be the same again. And strategic management is no exception to that. This great turbulence of the environment (of all the environments we have seen), these rapid and unpredictable changes it undergoes, will be a characteristic that companies will have to learn to live with. Whether there is a crisis or not, change is here to stay. As a result, strategic management must adapt to it. This obligation to think constantly about strategy is now permanent.

If this is so, we need strategic thinking models to help us, tools for thinking that take as their starting point other more general-purpose and complete models, such as the GIB model developed in the course of this book, to condense the key strategic aspects of a company. Using this strategic synthesis, it will be easier for the company to carry out daily monitoring of the strategy it pursues. More complete models (such as the GIB) can thus be left for moments of more in-depth thinking.

13.1 The Strategic Core: A Management Model in the Face of Complexity

In this chapter we present a new model, the strategic core,[1] as one of these new-generation tools, specially intended to allow this constant strategic monitoring in the face of extremely complex environments.

The strategic core sums up – extracts – the essence of the company's strategy, reducing it to a framework and four interrelated concepts. In this way it is much more straightforward to carry out this continuous monitoring. All the more so if we are conscious of the interrelation of these

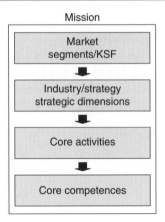

Figure 13.1   The strategic core (from the market to core competences)

concepts, since one leads to the next, like domino tiles that stand one next
to the other and only need the first to fall for the rest to follow suit.

As we can see in Figure 13.1, the strategic core is formed by the company's mission, the framework of the model, and inside this framework,
four interrelated strategic concepts: the market segments targeted by the
company, the strategy of the company (i.e. its strategic dimensions), its core
activities, and lastly its core competences.

13.2   Mission: The Framework of the Strategic Core

As was stressed in Chapter 2, the first thing a company must be clear about
is what it does, the nature of its business, what needs it satisfies, for whom,
and how – in a word, its mission. We saw that this is essential because
the company might realize that it has an outmoded business model, as in
the case related in that chapter, concerning Chrysler and General Motors,
which went bankrupt in summer 2009. The concepts contained within the
strategic core are of no consequence whatsoever if their framework (the
mission) does not stand up. Without a proper mission, the firm's future will
be very grim indeed.

But, as was also explained then, an appropriate business definition is
only a first *sine qua non* – except when the business model is absolutely
innovative, as was the case with Dell, Amazon and Swatch when they

started up. As we discussed, by having an innovative mission the company creates its own monopoly, insofar as it is the only company with that business definition. There can be no greater competitive advantage.

But these are exceptions; usually a company is forced to compete within that definition with other companies, all struggling to attract the same customers by satisfying the same needs. This is when it needs to find a competitive advantage, to be better than the rest of the companies in the industry in some aspect, naturally some aspect that is appreciated by its customers.

And out of this need to find a competitive advantage arise the four internal parts of the strategic core, as it is these four interrelated concepts that are responsible for earning the company its competitive advantage. All four are crucial, and all four are interrelated, because one leads on to the next, as we have already mentioned.

They are all necessary in order to achieve the ultimate strategic objective of the competitive advantage. Just as a soccer team needs a great goalkeeper, a very solid defense, exceptional midfield players and extraordinary forwards to win championships, the company needs all four strategic parts of the strategic core to be of a high standard. Just as a bad goalkeeper or a weak defense can cause a team with great players to lose a championship, it is enough for the firm to fall short of the optimal level in one of the four internal strategic concepts of the strategic core for failure to be assured.

13.3 The Four Concepts Inside the Framework of the Strategic Core

In the preceding chapters in this book we have described a wide variety of strategic concepts, all of them interrelated through the GIB model. The fundamental contribution of the strategic core is to select, out of all these concepts, which are essential for the constant monitoring of strategy, which concepts, and what relationships exist among them – in a word, to synthesize to the maximum the key elements of strategy. As we said earlier, this will help us to cope with the complexity facing companies at present. All the more so considering that if competitive advantage is very difficult to achieve it is even more difficult to maintain.

Any competitive advantage, no matter how strong and dominant it may be, has an expiry date, and shelf lives are getting shorter all the time. Therefore it is important to be constantly on the lookout against the possibility of losing one's competitive advantage, in order to reinforce it or change it before this happens. In 1999 General Motors headed the Fortune 500 list. In 2008 it ceased to be the biggest automobile manufacturer in the world.

At the beginning of 2009 it was bankrupt (only to be salvaged, albeit partially, by the Obama administration in summer 2009). Even the strongest competitive advantages evaporate, sometimes very quickly.

In short, only if senior managers know the key aspects of their strategy and monitor them constantly will they be able to try and keep ahead of the inexorable outdating of that strategy and the acceleration of that outdating as a result of the increasing complexity of the environment in which we live. Only if they have a clear understanding of why their customers buy from them, why they choose their firm, what it does better than the competition, can they hope to keep putting off that expiry date. This thinking about the synthesis of the key elements of strategy gives rise to these four internal concepts of the strategic core.

13.3.1   Market/Segments

Who are your customers? What do they value or need? Why do they buy from your company? We are unlikely to have to make much of an effort to defend the importance of these questions.[2] For this reason, the market is the first internal part of the strategic core. It is crucial for a company to be absolutely clear about who it targets, who its customers are, what needs of theirs it seeks to satisfy. Translating these vital concepts into the strategic concepts we have been discussing in this book, a company must identify what market segments it is targeting (there may be one or more than one) and what key success factors (KSFs) it seeks to satisfy in each of those segments.

In fact, we have already seen how a segment is defined on the basis of its KSFs. These key factors might be the appreciation of high quality, first-rate design, a select brand image, purchase through an exclusive distribution channel (and being willing to pay a very high price for it), in the case of someone who buys a handbag or some other accessory by Louis Vuitton, Hermes or Gucci. On the other hand, the KSF might simply be the appreciation of a reasonable price for a handbag or other accessory, in the case of someone with less purchasing power. Or someone might just attach less value to the quality, design and brand offered by these companies, and so be unwilling to pay the price they demand – even though on occasions one might have the purchasing power to do so.

This is key, because if a firm targets one segment or another, the remaining strategic concepts will all be totally different. In our example, the fact of having chosen two extremely distinct segments will make the remaining strategic concepts considerably different.

To sum up, as we stressed in Chapter 7, the market offers the company a menu of strategic possibilities (segments with their respective key factors), out of which the company has to decide which to choose, which segment or segments to target, in the knowledge that each of these segments has different needs to satisfy (which is precisely why they are different segments). This is the first internal link of the strategic core: the market, the segments of it targeted by the company (and the strategic decision not to target the rest).

In this respect, it must be borne in mind that, in turbulent times, what is valued by the various segments can change more rapidly than ever. And the relative importance of each segment – the number of customers in each segment and their potential to generate sales and profits – can change more rapidly still.

13.3.2 Industry/Strategic Dimensions

As we have already mentioned, one of the characteristics of the strategic core is that each of its parts, strategic concepts, leads to the next. Therefore, the market, the segments targeted by the company, will give us the keys to the next concept.

We have just seen how essential it is for the company to be clear about what segment it targets, what KSFs it seeks to satisfy. These same key factors will tell us what strategy the company should follow. This is the second internal link of the strategic core: the strategy of the company, the strategic dimensions it decides to aim at.

If, as in one of the examples we used earlier, a firm targets a segment whose customers value key factors such as high quality, first-rate design, a select brand image and exclusive distribution (commanding a very high price), these same KSFs tell us what strategy, what strategic dimensions, the company should have in order to be able to satisfy them. If we aim to satisfy customers who value high quality, first-rate design, a select brand image and exclusive distribution, what strategy will we follow? Logically, one aimed at achieving that high quality, first-rate design and select brand image, through an exclusive distribution channel.

What is the difference? The difference is that from the market perspective the high quality, first-rate design, select brand image and exclusive distribution are KSFs, as these are what the customer values, whereas from the industry perspective they are strategic dimensions, as this is what the company seeks to achieve; it is how it competes. Thus we see that market and industry, customers and the company, demand and supply, are like two concepts in front of a mirror; one is reflected in the other. As a result, one provides the key to the other; the segment and its KSFs tell us the company's strategy. KSFs lead to strategic dimensions.

We can trace this same step from market to industry with the other example we examined earlier. Think of the segment formed by customers who simply value price as a KSF. In this case, this market factor (low price) tells us that the company's strategic dimensions must be primarily cost-oriented, as its strategy will be focused on achieving an inexpensive product. Naturally, this strategy will fulfill the minimum standards demanded by the segment (what we have called minimum success factors). Yet while satisfying those minimum standards, the strategy will seek to achieve the largest possible cost savings. In comparison with the strategy described above, lower-quality materials will be used, fewer resources will be invested in design, distribution will be less exclusive, and so on.

This is why low-cost airlines eliminate unnecessary costs and the extras that characterize (although increasingly less so) traditional airlines. For example, they fly to cheaper, less busy airports; they do not supply free meals; they employ fewer crew; they have more seats (in the space left free by the crew and the meals); they operate more frequent flights (since they serve no meals they need less time to clean inside the airplanes); they use the Internet instead of travel agencies to cut distribution costs; and they maximize the use of their assets (their airplanes are flying for the maximum time possible). All these points are strategic dimensions aimed at obtaining a lower final cost – but, as always, fulfilling the minimum factors, in this case safety (above all) and punctuality.

Going back to Chapter 6, when we were thinking about the strategic dimensions of the company, we must bear in mind that it is not enough to be the best. Just as importantly, the company must be able to communicate this fact, convey it, because ultimately we live in a world of perceptions. Why are the brands Coca-Cola, McDonald's, Apple and Nike worth so much? True, they have good products, they do a good job of satisfying the needs they target, but there is much more value in the knowledge and perception of them that they have succeeded in producing in all of us. For this reason, one of the key strategic dimensions is nearly always the brand name, its image and its recognition.

13.3.3 Core Activities

The third link within the strategic core is formed by the core activities (areas, departments) of the company. As we discussed in Chapter 10, a company stakes its strategy on a small number of activities, not on all of them; this is an essential aspect of the competitive game. The firm cannot afford not to be the best at these activities. This is precisely what gives us the key to knowing which activities are fundamental. These activities are responsible for its strategy; they are vital to the company succeeding in carrying out its strategy.

We can see that, as always, the previous concept in the strategic core provides the clue to find the essence of the following one. Company strategy tells us which activities are core. The strategic dimensions indicate the essential areas of the organization. Continuing with the example of the strategy of companies such as Louis Vuitton, Hermes or Gucci, if their strategic dimensions were very high quality, design, brand image and an exclusive distribution channel, which areas of the company will undoubtedly be core areas? Those responsible for providing that very high quality, design, brand image and distribution.

Therefore, we can say that the departments of design and marketing are bound to be core areas in these cases. It is their responsibility to ensure that the company achieves its essential strategic dimensions. If the design department is not better than that of its competitors, the company will fail to obtain products with a better quality and design. If the marketing function is not superior to that of its competitors, its brand image and recognition will fall behind theirs. These companies have to deliver in these areas; for them they are core areas, and their strategy depends on them. Therefore, for its extreme importance, this is the third internal link in the strategic core.

Companies the likes of Louis Vuitton, Hermes or Gucci can, however, afford to be less than best in their industries in other activities. For example, they might not be the best at manufacturing. And since this is not a core area of theirs, they can consider the possibility of outsourcing it. If they are not the best they can think about another company performing this activity for them, as we saw in Chapter 10. Logically, it would have to be a company for which this is a core activity, an organization that does it very well. This is why many highly reputable firms in many industries (fashion, sport, cars, pharmaceuticals, drinks and many more) outsource their manufacturing. Because it is not a core area for them, because they do not do it better than the rest, they let experts in that function do it for them. Not only do they get a better performance; they also save resources that they can then invest in their core activities, which consequently they perform better, as we have explained.

Therefore, this is the third essential strategic concept that must always be followed. The core activities should focus the attention of the management team, as this is where strategy is fought out; it is the core activities that settle whether or not the competitive advantage is achieved.

13.3.4 Core Competences

How will we get the core activities performed better than those of our competitors? The answer is clear: by having better competences in them – by having better people (talent tends to be the fundamental strategic aspect, as we have already discussed), better technology and know-how, superior infrastructures or assets (e.g. facilities, machinery), better intangibles (e.g. brand image or recognition, market shares) and a greater financial capability, as we saw in Chapter 8. Again, in the strategic core one concept leads on to the next; it provides us with the crucial aspects of the following concept.

In the core activities, competences are essential because they either grant us or deny us the possibility of being better than our competitors in those areas. As we mentioned earlier, it is the intangible resources that usually make the difference. Aspects such as the skills of company staff, technology and reputation will provide the keys when we think about an organization's resources, about what its competitive advantage is based on. This is why Apple once dethroned IBM, despite the fact that it spent 100 times less on R&D than its competitor did.

In fact, intangible assets are much more difficult to imitate. And as we know, competitive advantage must be sustainable. This is why brand (its image and its recognition) is one of the strongest competitive advantages for many companies, as we have already discussed.

We have now completed the series of four concepts that make up the inside of the strategic core. Like pieces of a jigsaw puzzle fitting together, each of these concepts presents us with the next, and moreover provides us with the key to the competitive advantage of the company. We have seen this with the sequence market segments → strategic dimensions → core activities → core competences. From the market to competences, via strategy and activities.

Of course, if a company targets different segments, this succession of market segments → strategic dimensions → core activities → core competences is repeated separately and in parallel, as many times as segments the company wishes to satisfy. Logically, each segment will have different key factors. These will translate as different strategic dimensions. These in turn will lead to different core activities. And lastly, these will result in different competences. But we can always say that everything starts with the market, the segments the company decides to target.

13.4 Resource-based Strategy: the Reverse View of the Strategic Core

In Chapter 8 we introduced a strategic vision that is diametrically opposed to this market-based view of strategy: the resource-based view. This approach regards the company above all as an entity comprising core competences.

As the reader will recall, this approach holds that the key for strategy lies in resources, since the turbulence of the environment, its constant change, makes it very difficult for this environment to be taken as the foundation for the strategy of the company. In contrast, this view stresses that the firm's competences make a much more stable basis on which to define strategy. From this strategic perspective, the definition of the firm in terms of what it is capable of achieving, taking into account its resources, can offer a much sturdier foundation for defining strategy than one based on the variables that characterize the market.

If we think about the strategic core from this strategic vision, that of resources and competences, its same components are of use to us. The framework and the four key strategic concepts of the strategic core are still valid. They continue to sum up the basics of strategy, and its four stages continue to be interrelated. The difference lies in the strategic direction followed by its four internal concepts. From this strategic vision, the four internal stages of the core are analyzed in reverse order. In this case, it all starts with competences, which is where the strategic core ended up when we adopted the market-based view. The strategic order followed by the four internal concepts is the exact opposite.

As is shown in Figure 13.2, if we follow the perspective of this strategic approach and start the strategic core with competences, these will provide the essential information about activities. Depending on the nature of its competences, a company will be able to carry out certain (not all) activities better than the competition. These activities that are performed better than its competitors will indicate what sort of strategy – what strategic dimensions – the company can have as a competitive advantage. Finally, these strategic dimensions that the company masters better than the rest of the industry will show us which market segments the company can satisfy.

From this resource-based view, a company can understand that if it does not possess sufficient resources (people, know-how, assets, intangibles, money) to perform an activity really well, it will not do so better than the competition. Hence it will not obtain superior strategic dimensions, and consequently it will fail to satisfy its customers' needs better than its

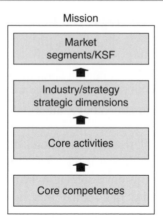

Figure 13.2 The strategic core from the resource-based view

competitors do, a *sine qua non*. The resource-based view enables the company to see clearly whether it will be capable of carrying out a strategy better than its competitors.

Returning to our earlier example of companies of the sort typified by Louis Vuitton, Hermes and Gucci, if a firm in their industry wished to imitate their strategy, from this perspective it might realize that it has neither the staff nor the knowledge, nor the prestige, nor the financial resources of these companies. It would see clearly that it falls short of their standards in regard to competences. In this way it would be obvious to it that it would be unable to perform the core activities of design and marketing to the same standards as these companies. This would then lead it to deduce that it would be incapable of achieving the basic strategic dimensions in their strategy. It could not attain the same level of design, brand and distribution as the firms described. And so it would conclude that it could not satisfy the segments of consumers that appreciate all these key factors better than they do.

Consequently, as we have already put forward, the resource-based view of the strategic core makes it absolutely clear to the company whether it will be capable of performing a given strategy better than its competitors. If the conclusion is negative, the best thing a company can do is to look for another strategy.

This is not to say that this firm should forget about the possibility. It should always be borne in mind that strategy is dynamic, it changes by the second, especially when the complexity of the environment increases. Perhaps today this strategy is beyond the company's reach. Maybe today is not the day to attack Louis Vuitton, Hermes or Gucci. But as we have also described in this book, there is such a thing as vision. This company may not be able to perform this strategy today, it may have insufficient competences, but it can have the vision of doing so. And if it does, and it works to one day gain the competences it now lacks, in the future it might get this reverse chain of core competences → core activities → strategic dimensions → market segments to yield a positive result.

13.5 Reality: Merging The Two Logics of the Strategic Core

We have just described the strategic core model, which follows two opposing directions: one based on the view of strategy in which the market takes precedence, and the other built on the resource-based view of strategy. If we think about these two opposing visions of strategy we can go a little further. We can imagine that the market-based view is an approach that is better suited to analysis, thinking, seeing strategic possibilities; hence we start with a menu of possibilities in the market. On the other hand, the resource-based view is more a decision-making perspective, for facing the harsh reality of being what we are, seeing what our company can actually do with all the possibilities detected in the analysis. Figure 13.3 shows the logic of both approaches.

The two approaches to the strategic core are equally rational, although they work in opposite directions. As we explain above, each direction makes more sense at a particular strategic moment, depending whether we are

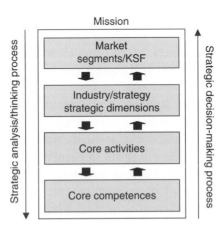

Figure 13.3 The two logics, the two directions of the strategic core

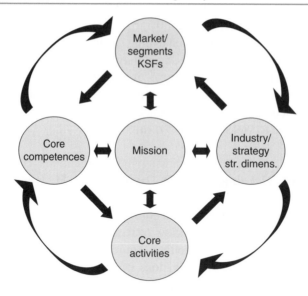

Figure 13.4 The strategic core reflecting the merging of its two logics

analysing or deciding; whether we are thinking or resolving. However, business reality cannot separate stages so neatly. The theory of the formulation process followed by the implementation process gives way to a reality that blends the two, due to the absolute turbulence of today's environments.

The complexity of the environment in which we move forces us into a constant dynamic of thinking-acting where these two directions permanently interact, as depicted in Figure 13.4. This figure of the strategic core is perhaps the closest match to the present reality, as it reflects the five components of the model with its two simultaneous directions, thus emphasizing still further the total interrelation of all its components.

This new figure of the strategic core continues to highlight the logical predominance of the mission as the axis around which the model revolves. It is logical because, as we have explained, the mission defines the business, and a change in the mission will result in changes in all the other concepts in the strategic core. We should bear in mind that it is for this reason that the mission is the framework of the strategic core. And it is why in this new figure it occupies a central position around which the rest of the concepts move like planets around the sun. When the sun stops giving off its huge supply of heat, the planets will die. Similarly, an outmoded business model has no survivors.

Reality is too complex to follow clearly separate rules and stages. Reality leads us to a constant balancing act between the two directions, between thinking and decision-making, between the market-based view and the resource-based view. This same reality has erased the once clear and sharp separation between formulating and implementing strategy. If nowadays companies are in a constant merged process of formulation and implementation, obviously these two directions of the strategic core intertwine – among other reasons, because the environment is so fickle that what we could call the strategic management circle is never closed. There is constant feedback between the formulation and the implementation of strategy.

Thus the strategic core as we see it depicted in Figure 13.4 is the best expression of the essence of strategic management. It sets forth the key concepts and how they are interrelated, but implying that both directions are logical. Either of them may be the most appropriate at a particular moment. But above all it shows the importance of taking into account the state of these concepts at all times, as the situation of any of them can change when least expected.

Strategic management as of the second decade of the twenty-first century is rather like Formula One driving. In this type of racing, the driver can never take his eyes off the circuit, or cease paying attention to either his rivals' cars or all the essential indicators in his own car. Competition is extreme every second. Everything can change on account of the weather conditions (the environment) or the action of a rival (competitor). Racing conditions differ depending on the various parts of the circuit (segments), to which the driver must adapt with precision. Needless to say, the driver's car (capabilities) must always be the best – and not even Ferrari can always manage that.

Business competition today is similar. Hence entrepreneurs and managers need clear synthetic tools enabling them first to understand at all times the complex situation in which they operate, and then on this basis to react as rapidly as possible, as time is often the only thing they lack. In strategic management, the relaxing times when they drove a little runabout, and even had time to admire the countryside, will never return.

13.6 Questions for Reflection

I. Given the characteristics of your industry, do you think a model like the strategic core might be of use to you?

II. What is the mission of your company?[3] Is your business model the right one? How long do you think it will continue to be so?

III. How many sequences of the four internal concepts of the strategic core occur in your company? In other words, how many market segments does your company target?

IV. Describe each of the internal sequences of the strategic core in the case of your organization:

     a. Market segment

     b. Strategic dimensions

     c. Core activity/activities

     d. Core competences

V. Value each of these sequences: Segment $\leftarrow \rightarrow$ Dimensions $\leftarrow \rightarrow$ Core activity/activities $\leftarrow \rightarrow$ Core competences. In each of them, do you think they provide your company with a significant competitive advantage? Why? For how long do you think it will be sustainable?

VI. Ask yourself the last four questions again, but this time thinking about the future strategy of your company. What changes do you visualize in your company's strategic core in the future? What are your reasons for thinking that these changes will be necessary?

VII. Describe the changes, in regard to both the mission and the various sequences that either already exist or may appear in the future:

     a. Market segment

     b. Strategic dimensions

     c. Core activity/activities

     d. Core competences

GUIDE TO BOOK CHAPTERS THROUGH THE GIB MODEL

In Figure G.1 the GIB model is numbered with the chapters of the book that deal with each of its concepts (Chapters 1, 12 and 13 do not deal with any specific concept of the GIB model).

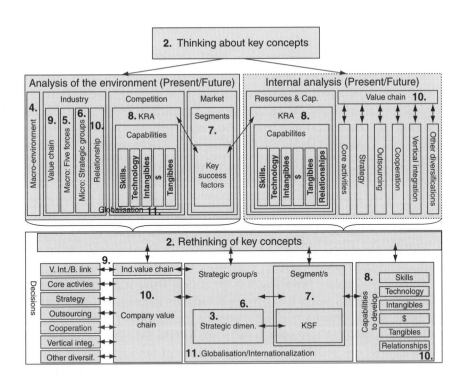

Figure G.1 The GIB model showing the chapters of the book that deal with each of its concepts

ACKNOWLEDGMENTS

This is a difficult chapter. Inevitably, some people will be overlooked. Any work is the outcome of countless interactions throughout one's life, and it is impossible to remember them all. Moreover, it is often impossible to make one's words reflect one's thanks to certain key individuals.

First of all, I would like to extend special thanks to Lluís Carbonell and Jordi Fortuny for reviewing the text and introducing improvements. Also to Professors Amy Leaverton and Simon Dolan for their encouragement and assistance in bringing the book to fruition.

I would never have come to write this book were it not for ESADE, as it has given me the opportunity to improve day by day for more than 20 intense professional years. I have received crucial support from its directors general over this period, Dr Jaume Filella, Dr Lluís Maria Pugès (also my first dean), Dr Carlos Losada and Dr Eugenia Bieto, and from the Director of ESADE Argentina, Dr Alejandro Bernhardt. The support of the Deans of Management of these years, Dr Lluís Maria Pugès, Dr Robert Tornabell, Dr Xavier Mendoza and Dr Alfons Sauquet, has likewise been essential. No less stalwart has been the support lent by the Directors of Executive Education over this time, Professor Pedro Sepúlveda, Dr Carlos Gallucci and Professor Jaume Hugas. Neither can I forget the Heads of the Department of Business Policy, Professor Antoni Aliana, Dr Marcel Planellas and Professor Montse Ollé.

Over these years I have learnt a great deal from many ESADE professors. In my early years I was overwhelmed by the extraordinary human and professional grandeur of professors of the stature of Adolf Vilanova and Carles Comas. Years later, I have yet to find the words to describe, and to express my gratitude for, the experience of researching and writing my doctoral dissertation under the supervision of experts of the academic and personal qualities of Josep Bisbe and Joan Manuel Batista. I also had the immense luck to be able to write papers together with them and with someone of the intellectual solvency of Xavier Mendoza. I had many intense and fascinating professional experiences with Jordi Molina. I worked with such exceptional people as Alberto Gimeno, Carles Torrecilla, Carles Roig, Dolors Carreño, Joan Roig, Jordi Brunat, José M. Alvarez de Lara, Josep Lluís Cano, Josep Franch, Lourdes Teixidor, Santiago Simón, Rodrigo Rama and Xavier Mena. Even without my working with them, many other great ESADE professors influenced me; to name them would practically be tantamount to copying the list of the entire faculty of the school.

The experience of working for long periods of time with great entrepreneurs and managers has also been fundamental in bringing this book to completion. Working in collaboration with people such as Juan Vilella, Ferran Roca-Cusachs, Antoni Colell, Jordi Belloc, Alex Morales, Constanza Palomino, Manuel Ferrer and Federico Ast leaves an indelible mark.

This book has also been influenced by a great non-managerial professional, the journalist Ramón Besa. Through his friendship and professionalism he has transmitted extremely important values to me, together with the keys to a job well done.

I would like to thank Palgrave Macmillan for publishing this book, and especially Stephen Rutt, its Global Publishing Director, who believed in it from the start. This English version also owes much to its translator, Toby Willett, who did his job with great skill and professionalism.

I will always be indebted to my parents, my brother and my sister for having shown me the right way through example. Lastly, there are no words to express my thanks to my family for the innumerable weekends and public holidays that this book in particular and my professional life in general has deprived them of. Without their understanding and support none of this would have been possible.

Notes

Introduction

1. GIMBERT, Xavier. *El enfoque estratégico de la empresa.* Ediciones Deusto, Bilbao, 1998; GIMBERT, Xavier. *El futur de l'empresa.* Columna Edicions-Edicions Proa, Barcelona 1998. GIMBERT, Xavier et al. *Como elaborar un plan estratégico en la empresa.* Cuadernos Cinco Días, Madrid, 1999.

2. GIMBERT, Xavier, BISBE, Josep & MENDOZA, Xavier. "The role of performance measurement systems in strategy formulation processes", *Long Range Planning*, August 2010, 43(4), 477–497; GIMBERT, Xavier. "El núcleo estratégico como modelo de gestión ante la complejidad", *Harvard-Deusto Business Review*, September 2009, 182, 36–48. AST, Federico & GIMBERT, Xavier. "La Selección Francesa de Fútbol Crónica de un desastre de management anunciado". *Harvard Deusto Business Review.* December 2010, 196, 22–36.

I Strategic Management, Strategic Levels and Processes

1. ANSOFF, Igor. *Corporate strategy*, McGraw-Hill, New York, 1965.

2. OCASIO, W. & JOSEPH, J. "Rise and fall – or transformation? The evolution of strategic planning at the General Electric Company, 1940–2006", *Long Range Planning*, 41, 2008.

3. ANSOFF, Igor. *Corporate strategy*, McGraw-Hill, New York, 1965.

4. MINTZBERG, Henry. "Patterns of strategy formulation", *Management Science*, 24, 1978; QUINN, J.B. *Strategies for change: logical incrementalism*, Irwin, Homewood, IL, 1980.

5. MINTZBERG, Henry and WATERS, J.A. "Of strategies, deliberate and emergent", *Strategic Management Journal*, 6, 1985, pp. 257–272.

6. MINTZBERG, Henry. "The design school: reconsidering the basic premises of strategic management", *Strategic Management Journal*, 11, 3, 1990, pp. 171–195; ANSOFF, Igor. "Critique of Henry Mintzberg's 'The design school: reconsidering the basic premises of strategic management", *Strategic Management Journal*, 12, 6, 1991, pp. 449–461; MINTZBERG, Henry. "Learning 1, Planning 0: reply to Igor Ansoff", *Strategic Management Journal*, 12, 6, 1991, pp. 463–466.

7. GRANT, Robert. "Strategic planning in a turbulent environment: evidence from the oil majors", *Strategic Management Journal*, 24, 2003, pp. 491–517.

2 Key Strategic Concepts

1. This method of presenting the key concepts in the form of a sculpture was drawn up in the 1980s by Adolf Vilanova, professor of business policy at ESADE.

2. ABELL, Derek F. *Defining the business: the starting point of strategic planning*, Prentice Hall, Englewood Cliffs, NJ, 1980.

3 Competitive Advantage and Strategy

1. In 1997 Guinness PLC and Grand Metropolitan PLC merged to form Diageo PLC, thus constituting the world's leading premium beverage corporation. In addition to Guinness, Diageo includes brands such as Smirnoff, Johnnie Walker, Baileys, J&B, Tanqueray, Crown Royal and Sterling Vineyards, among others.

2. To quote the leaflets Guinness hand out to visitors at the Dublin brewery: "Arthur's formula was deceptively simple. He took four basic ingredients – hops, water, barley and yeast …".

3. PORTER, Michael. *Competitive Advantage: Creating and Sustaining Superior Pperformance*, Free Press, New York, 1985.

4. SEGARRA, Toni. *Desde el otro lado del escaparate*, Espasa Calpe, Madrid, 2009.

5. PUELLES, J.A. and PUELLES, M. "Marcas de distribuidor: 100 ideas clave. Distribución y consumo", *Mercasa*, Madrid, July–August 2009.

6. MUÑOZ, Ramón. "Low cost", *El País*, 11 August 2009.

5 Industry Analysis (1): Macro

1. PORTER, Michael. *Competitive strategy*, The Free Press, New York, 1980.

2. The order of presentation of the five forces here is the author's decision in view of the story used to illustrate them. This does not mean that the five forces are ordered, or that each of them occupies a place in that distribution.

3. This question is related to the definition of your mission in section 2.9.

4. Again, a change in the industry definition will imply a change in the mission.

6 Industry Analysis (II): Micro

1. Stout is a thick, very black beer with plenty of body. It is has a bitter flavor and a roasted quality as a result of the roasted malts used in making it.

2. Beamish was founded in 1792, while Murphy's was set up in 1856.

3. PORTER, Michael. *Competitive strategy*, chap. 5.

4. An advertisement from the year 2000 by the agency Lautrec Euro RSCG for the Argentinean business magazine *Mercado*.

5. FRANCH, J., GIMBERT, X. and CANO, J.L. "Raventós i Blanc at a Crossroads", case study, 2009.

6. The names of the companies in the industry have been omitted given the fact, discussed earlier, that competitive position is dynamic. When the reader sees the figure, the position of the various named companies could be different from that found at

the time of writing. Furthermore, the figure has been simplified, as it is only intended as an example of this tool.

7. See Section 4.6 of Chapter 4.

7 Market Analysis

1. PUELLES, J.A. and PUELLES, M. "Marcas de distribuidor: 100 ideas clave, distribución y consumo", Mercasa, Madrid, July–August 2009.

2. See Section 6.6 in the previous chapter.

8 Resources and Capabilities

1. OHMAE, Kenichi. *The mind of the strategist*, McGraw-Hill, New York, 1978.

2. Key result areas will be called core activities when we are analysing the company's value chain perspective.

3. ULRICH, D., VON GLINOW, M.A. and JICK, T. "High-impact learning: building and diffusing learning capability", *Organizational Dynamics*, 1993.

4. JOHNSON, G., SCHOLES, K. and WHITTINGTON, R. *Exploring corporate strategy*, Financial Times, Prentice Hall, NJ, 2008.

5. WERNERFELT, Birger. "A resource-based view of the firm", *Strategic Management Journal*, 1984.

6. WERNERFELT, Birger. "A resource-based view of the firm: ten years after", *Strategic Management Journal*, 1995.

7. QUINN, J.B. *Intelligent enterprise*, Free Press, New York, 1992.

8. GRANT, R.M. "The resource-based theory of competitive advantage: implications for strategy formulation", *California Management Review*, 1991.

9. HAMEL, Gary and PRAHALAD, C.K. "The core competence of the corporation", *Harvard Business Review*, 1990.

9 Industry Value Chain

1. The concept of the value chain was first defined by the consultancy firm McKinsey, although they used the term "business system" in 1980 to refer to the company value chain, as developed in the next chapter.

2. In backward integration, the company or industry becomes a competitor of its suppliers.

10 Company Value Chain

1. As mentioned above, page 127, note 1. See BALES, C., CHATTERJEE, P., GOGEL, D. and PURI, A. *Competitive cost analysis*, McKinsey & Company internal document. GLUCK, Frederick W. 'Strategic choices and research allocation,' *The McKinsey Quarterly*, 1980.

2. PORTER, Michael. *Competitive advantage: creating and sustaining superior performance*, chap. 3.

3. As explained in that chapter, in note 2.

4. The Swatch Group comprises 19 brands of watches, and targets all market segments, from luxury (Breguet, Blancpain, Glashütte Original, Jaquet Droz, Léon Hatot, Omega, Tiffany & Co.) to basic (Swatch, Flik Flak), through the high (Longines, Rado, Union Glashütte) and middle ranges (Tissot, ck, Balmain, Certina, Mido, Hamilton). It also includes Endura, which makes watches for brands in other industries (e.g. Timberland and Mango).

5. This is one of its advantages; others are the high concentration of the industry, in which Grifols became leader after taking over Talecris Biotherapeutics in June 2010, and also the long period required to install new capacity (at least five years).

6. Industries as diverse as airlines, fitness centers, cell phones, music, finance and soft drinks.

7. This question is the same as the one we asked in Section 8.5 when thinking about the company's capabilities. Therefore, the answer will be the same.

11 Globalization, Strategy, and Internationalization

1. LEVITT, Theodore. "The globalization of markets", *Harvard Business Review*, May 1983.

2. Adapted from YIP, G.S. *Total global strategy, managing for worldwide competitive advantage*, Prentice Hall, Englewood Cliffs, NJ, 1992.

3. It is the No. 1 imported beer in the USA and No. 1 Mexican beer in the world.

4. IMMELT, J., GOVINDARAJAN, V. and TRIMBLE, C. "How GE is disrupting itself", *Harvard Business Review*, October 2009.

5. JARILLO, José Carlos and MARTÍNEZ, Jon. *Estrategia internacional*, chap. 4, McGraw-Hill, Madrid, 1991.

6. *Clarín*. Buenos Aires, 22 May 2009.

7. *El Universal*. Mexico City, 4 August 2009.

8. JOHANSON, J. and VAHLNE, J.E. "The mechanism of internationalization", *International Marketing Review*, 1990.

9. ALONSO, J.A. "El proceso de internacionalización de la empresa. Información Comercial Española", *Revista de Economía*, January 1994.

10. JARILLO and MARTÍNEZ, *Estrategia internacional*.

11. VIVES, L. and MENDOZA, X. *La expansión de la multinacional española: Estrategias y cambios organizativos*. Observatorio de la Empresa Multinacional Española, Madrid, 2008.

12. JOHNSON, G., SCHOLES, K. and WHITTINGTON, R. *Exploring corporate strategy*, chap. 8.

12 Strategy and Crisis

1. MANGELSDORF, Martha E. "Good days for disruptors", *MIT Sloan Management Review*, spring 2009, 50, 3, pp. 67–70.

2. RUMELT, Richard P. "Strategy in a 'structural break'", *McKinsey Quarterly*, January–March 2009, Issue 1, pp. 35–42.

3. GOVINDARAJAN, Vijay. "Preparing for the recovery", *The Wall Street Journal*, 22 June 2009.

4. ARTHUR D. Little. *Beyond the downturn: Waking up in a new world*, April 2009.

5. KPMG. *Never catch a falling knife*, June 2009.

6. *El País*, 1 December 1996.

7. Large business conglomerate in industries such as airlines, telecommunications, music, gyms, drinks, radio stations and others; it even includes the first company to offer trips into space, Virgin Galactic.

13   The Strategic Core Model

1. GIMBERT, Xavier. "El núcleo estratégico como modelo de gestión ante la complejidad", *Harvard Deusto Business Review*, September 2009, Vol. 182, pp. 36–48.

2. We will not go back over concepts that we have already explained in previous chapters; here our intention is simply to focus on why they are considered essential, why they form part of the strategic core. Furthermore, we will describe the relationship that exists between them.

3. This question is the same as that asked in Section 2.9.

INDEX

Note: Page numbers followed by letter '*f*' refers to figures.